Self-Esteem
The Way of Humility

Jennifer Minney

with illustrations by
Brian Minney

Silvertree Publishing

Published 2000
by
Silvertree Publishing
PO Box 2768, Yeovil, Somerset

ISBN: 0-9538446-2-5

Printed and bound by
Redwood Books, Trowbridge

Dedication

To my husband, whose constant love and encouragement over the years have been the means of enhancing my own self-esteem.

Contents

Author's Note

For the sake of clarity, the masculine pronoun "he" has been used throughout the book, although the text is equally, and in some cases more, applicable to women. Similarly, the biblical "man" has been used, according to its original meaning, to denote all of humankind.

Preface

Low self-esteem is a problem that I have encountered again and again during my long counselling career, for the US army in Germany, and for the NHS and in private practice in England. I have discovered it to be at the root of most, if not all, problems: depression, anxiety, stress, marital difficulties.... Therefore, it is a subject that has long interested me — and not only because of my counselling work. It is a problem that I too have struggled with.

I should never have been born in the first place — or so my physically abusive parents kept telling me. And from the start I was a disappointment to them. They wanted a boy; I was a girl. Mum wanted me to be blonde like her; I was dark. Dad wanted me to be a wiz at maths; I preferred writing poetry. And, when I left school, he forced me to work in accounting, although I really wanted to read literature at university. This he forbade because, he said, I was only a girl, and girls were too stupid to learn.

The repair and development of my own damaged self-esteem really began when I came to Christ and joined a caring and supportive church. And the healing process was accelerated when I acquired the confidence to attend Bible College, to train for ministerial work, and graduated "with distinction". But it was my husband, whom I met during subsequent nursing training, who maintained and deepened the healing. His love gave me the freedom to be myself, to develop my own interests and talents in my own time and in my own way, so that eventually I was able to realise my dream of going to university. I graduated from the University of Maryland, European Division, with a BA in Psychology (with Literature as my minor subject), Summa cum Laude; that is, with the highest honours. And, I won a special award, being the top graduate in Europe. I had proved my father wrong, although he had long since died and wasn't there to see it.

My professional experience, in a variety of spheres, and my own struggles and achievements, have led me to view self-esteem as part of the broader picture of spiritual and psycho-logical growth. For this reason, this book has taken a different approach to the usual books on the subject. Not only is there an interweaving of insights from Christian teaching and modern psychology, but strands from other areas of knowledge have also been incorporated, creating greater colour and depth.

This is a book about personal development in all areas of life — social, mental, physical, emotional and spiritual. It is about opening up, like a flower, to the light of God's love and, through that love, discovering our unique strengths and abilities, and realising our true potential.

Jennifer Minney BA, SRN, SCM

1

Introduction and Overview

CHRISTIANS AND SELF-ESTEEM

Why Christians suffer from low self-esteem

The Christian message is a message of love. It is the good news that, however bad we feel about ourselves, God wants to welcome us into his family, to give us a sense of belonging, and an assurance of our worth.

Many respond to this message because it is precisely what they need: they feel worthless and unloved, with nowhere to turn, and they want to experience, perhaps for the first time, what love is all about. As self-esteem is linked with the assurance of being lovable and loved, with the ability to love in return, it follows that the Christian Church is full of people who have — or have had — low self-esteem.

Although God's love is there from the start, healthy self-esteem does not suddenly come into existence the moment we turn to him. It comes with spiritual maturity. We have to grow into the knowledge of God, becoming increasingly more acquainted with his character and ways of working. But sadly, the very feelings of hurt and rejection that may have brought us to God in the first place can prevent spiritual growth, however much it is sought after. We grow and blossom in God, becoming more self-assured and confident, only as we are able to open up to his love. And if there has been a history of abuse or rejection, if love is viewed with suspicion and mistrust, it is very difficult to respond to love — or even recognise it.

In addition, many Christians continue to struggle with self-esteem problems because of misunderstanding about how we are meant to view ourselves. Self-esteem is often confused with selfishness, and self-love with self-seeking. There may also be misunderstanding about the changes that occur when we come to Christ. If we expect a change of personality, or to find that all our problems, including self-esteem ones, are solved, then discovering that we still feel the same about ourselves can lead to guilt. And guilt lowers self-esteem even further.

To some degree, everyone has self-esteem problems. We all have difficulty accepting some parts of ourselves, and we all lack confidence in some situations. And no one can claim to have perfect love or unwavering trust. Also, whatever our experience of God and our reasons for coming to him — or rejecting him — we all struggle, at least sometimes, with feelings of worthlessness; of not being loved unconditionally. So everyone needs to work at enhancing self-esteem. The first step is to begin clearing away any misunderstandings, clarifying just what it means to be a Christian, and the effect this has on self-esteem.

The effects of becoming a Christian

Becoming a Christian means that, rather than there being a change of personality, or the elimination of all self-esteem problems, there is a change of status: from being alienated from God to becoming his children. We may not be ideal children, but we are, nevertheless, God's children; members of his family who can come to him at any time without fear. The apostle Paul wrote, "For you did not receive a spirit that makes you a slave again to fear, but you received the Spirit of sonship." [1]

There is also a change of disposition. There is a new tendency towards God, and a new desire to please him. And we are now able to please him because, through Christ's sacrificial death, we are set free from the power of sin — and from the old patterns of perceiving ourselves as worthless, unlovable and unloved. This new freedom doesn't mean that we become sinless, or that the old patterns simply disappear. Being human we continue to make a mess of things. But we are no longer held back by a fear of judgement and condemnation, so we can work more effectively at changing the old, destructive ways of coping with life's problems: "Therefore, there is now no condemnation for those who are in Christ Jesus...." [2]

10

Finally, with repentance — a prerequisite for becoming a Christian — there is a change of direction. We turn away from the old life and start heading towards spiritual health and fulfilment. This is an instantaneous turn-around, but it takes time to "Produce fruit in keeping with repentance." [3]

In order to produce fruit, the ground first has to be cleared, and when there has been a childhood of abuse and rejection, this is especially hard. It also takes time for misunderstandings to be fully cleared away, and to learn how to trust and benefit from the love that God is longing to shower upon us. Accepting Christ as Saviour and Lord is just the beginning. Seeing oneself in a new, healthy way, and learning to love and esteem oneself, is part of a developmental process that ultimately will take a lifetime. Fruits do not grow and ripen overnight. So, be patient with yourself.

Before you set off in the new direction of healthy self-esteem, it will help if you have some idea of how you came to have self-esteem problems in the first place. It is particularly important that you recognise that your failures and difficulties may have arisen, not primarily because of any inadequacies in your own personality, but because others have failed you. This is not with the purpose of allocating blame, but in order to better understand yourself and your difficulties.

WHERE SELF-ESTEEM COMES FROM

Our family

The story of our self begins at conception — possibly before. It is then that the pattern is laid down for our self-concept (how we perceive ourselves), and our self-esteem (how we feel about ourselves). A baby is affected, for better or worse, by the mother's feelings about it during pregnancy, by how the mother feels about herself, and by what is going on in her life generally. But perhaps of primary importance is how our parents felt about our arrival. An unwanted pregnancy is not necessarily an unwanted baby. But when a parent continues to have negative or ambivalent feelings about a baby's arrival, or about its gender, or some imperfection — such as being handicapped — the baby

11

senses the parent's feelings. And the result, unless there are other loving family members to compensate, such as grandparents, is a negative, rejecting view of the self.

Our position in the family also has a bearing on self-esteem. The eldest, or an only child, is often given more responsibility, which may make him feel important and needed; although if too much is expected the result can be frustration and a persistent feeling of failure. The youngest, on the other hand, often has little or no responsibility, and since the parents are usually in a better position to afford material things, the youngest has a better chance of fulfilling his ambitions and dreams. But the tendency of parents, and older siblings, to treat the youngest as the baby of the family, and to dismiss or even ridicule his thoughts and feelings, may lead to a feeling of inferiority. The middle child can often feel lost, not quite knowing where he belongs in the family hierarchy, so he may grow up with a poor sense of identity.

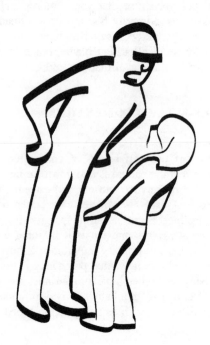

Any negative effects accruing from our position in the family are exacerbated when there is also a persistent lack of love, or if love has not been demonstrated. Children who have been deprived of physical affection, who have grown up feeling unloved and unwanted, find it very difficult to love themselves, especially if they have also been constantly criticised, put down, ridiculed, told that they are ugly or stupid, or that they will never amount to anything. How parents express love includes how they discipline. Discipline that is too lax, with too much freedom allowed, is as unloving and detrimental to self-esteem as discipline that is too harsh or boundaries that are too rigid.

Our schools

Our experience of school also plays a part in setting the pattern of self-esteem. We are affected, not only by how our parents judged our performance, and by how much they encouraged or criticised, but also by how our teachers judged us. Children naturally want to please, and when they feel that they consistently fail to measure up, their self-esteem is eroded. Also of importance is the methods teachers used to instil learning: whether teaching was unimaginative or creative, harsh or gentle, and whether or not it allowed for individual interests and abilities.

The development of self-esteem is also affected by our experience of other children during the school years. Especially harmful is being made to feel different, through being repeatedly excluded from friendship circles, teased — about such things as weight, or wearing glasses — or bullied.

Society in general

The patterns for self-esteem are also laid down by society in general, especially in this modern era when children have so much exposure to societal values and standards, primarily through television, but increasingly through the internet. Such things as soaps and advertising can have a subtle effect on a child's development, making him feel that he doesn't measure up; that he's not as clever, attractive, or as well-off as others. Exposure to the media creates a tendency to compare, and we usually come off worse. The influence of society, including our schools or clubs, interacts with that of our parental home, modifying, for better or worse, the effects on our developing sense of self.

Self-esteem problems may, of course, develop in later life, through, for example, being constantly criticised or demeaned by a spouse or senior work colleague. But if the foundations are sound, the damage will not be pervasive and recovery will be relatively straightforward. On the other hand, when there is already low self-esteem, later erosion of one's sense of worth can be devastating.

Since there are so many causes of low self-esteem, and we are such complex beings, it may be difficult for you, if your childhood was essentially a happy one, to work out just where your self-esteem problems came from. The task is complicated by the fact that different things affect different people in different ways. For example, a sensitive, imaginative child will be more adversely affected by destructive criticism than a more outgoing child. Begin, then, by identifying what, of the above, applies to you, adding anything that may have been omitted. Then note those things that troubled you the most. Again, this is not in order to apportion blame, but to put the responsibility where it belongs. This is particularly important if you have experienced abuse of any kind.

Abuse victims tend to blame themselves for their ill-treatment, and if you are still doing this, start telling yourself that you were not to blame, and that it was not your shame. This is the beginning of breaking the patterns of low self-esteem, because any feelings of badness or worthlessness arising from childhood trauma can lead to problems in adulthood that will lower self-esteem even further.

THE EFFECTS OF LOW SELF-ESTEEM

A distorted view of oneself

Low self-esteem leads to a distorted view of oneself: we don't see ourselves as we really are. We may see ourselves as worthless, unloved and unlovable, ugly, stupid, ineffective, incompetent.... And inevitably, we become what we think we are. We become prickly and defensive, making it hard for people to love us; we put up barriers so that no-one can get close to us; we neglect our appearance or dress dowdily in order to hide perceived ugliness, so we don't look our best; and if we are able to accept challenges, we perform poorly.

A distorted view of others

Low self-esteem also leads to a distorted and pessimistic view of others, and the world in general. For example, we may see others as unkind, unfriendly, stupid, irritating, disapproving, superior.... These misperceptions, in turn, lead to our avoiding company, or acting superciliously or aggressively, with the result that people really do become unfriendly; or, through fear of our anger, behave stupidly. The end result is lack of friends, failed marriages, and an inability to function efficiently in a work setting.

A distorted view of God

Low self-esteem also leads to a distorted view of God. We may know the Bible and know in our minds that God is loving and kind, and yet live in fear of his disapproval and not be able to feel close to him. And, in order to compensate for feelings of insecurity, we may develop a rigid belief system, so we become slaves to the letter of the law rather than experiencing the freedom that is ours through Christ. On the other hand, we may create an idealised Father Christmas-type God who lets us have everything we want. This misperception also leads to a sense of alienation because feeling loved includes feeling safe, and we cannot feel safe without firm boundaries. With all these distortions there is stunted spiritual growth and development, which further prevents the development of healthy self-esteem.

In order to gain a healthy sense of self, you will find it helpful to not only mark those areas where you are most struggling — the questionnaire at the end of this book will help you with this — but also to identify your goals: how you would like to be and what you would like to achieve. You will reach your destination quicker if you know where you're heading — and if you find the best starting place.

THE BASIS FOR HEALTHY SELF-ESTEEM

A true awareness of what self-esteem is

People often talk about self-esteem without being able to give any consistent definition of what it actually is. It is generally considered to be self-confidence: a belief in one's abilities to achieve and relate to others. Or, it is perceived as an assurance of one's own worth and integrity. Both of these are true. But it is so much more.

Before Adam sinned he had perfect self-esteem. But after the Fall he no longer had the assurance of being of value to God, or of being accepted, approved and loved. And so he hid from God's presence. True self-esteem means that we don't have to hide from God, from other people, or from ourselves. It can be summarised as the confidence to approach God just as we are,

16

perfectly assured of our welcome at all times. This, in turn, leads to the confidence to face the world.

When we have this kind of self-esteem, we have a realistic perception of ourselves; there is an awareness of weaknesses and failures, but also of our abilities, strengths and achievements. So we are able to be spontaneous, open and friendly, and we can get close to people. We also feel good about the way we look and make the most of ourselves. We are able to accept challenges, and we generally perform well. A healthy self-esteem also leads to a realistic view of others; we don't expect too much or too little, so we are able to form good relationships. And, we have a realistic, and basically optimistic, view of the world in general. There is also a healthy concept of God, so we are able to trust God in all circumstances, feel loved and valued by him, and be able to love him in return. We no longer perceive God as just someone out there, but also as someone within — a part of us.

A true awareness of God in us

Attaining high self-esteem according to worldly principles, as propounded by some psychological theories, can lead to a false sense of worth. What is termed self-esteem may actually be conceit or pride, or a feeling of superiority. The world teaches that man is the centre of the universe, and that a person can develop a healthy self-concept and high self-esteem through his own efforts; that is, through discovering a self that is essentially divorced from God. But the psychological and spiritual are integral, therefore a person cannot truly discover his own psyche (soul) without also discovering the divinity within.

God made us with an innate sense of the divine. "He has made everything beautiful in its time. He has also set eternity in the hearts of men; yet they cannot fathom what God has done from beginning to end." [4] It follows, then, that knowing one's true self leads to a greater knowledge of God. But basing a knowledge of God only on the basis of self-discovery is potentially dangerous. We must seek first and foremost to know God, and through knowing God discover, and become increasingly in tune with, our own true selves. God is our best starting place.

A true awareness of our identity in God

Having begun in God, basing our self-esteem on a knowledge and awareness of God in us, we continue by becoming increasingly aware of our identity in God. We are God's children, created in his image and redeemed (bought back) through his love. There can be no greater sense of self-worth than that which comes from knowing, with absolute assurance, that we are children and heirs of God.

Self-esteem is also based on our identity as a chosen people, with royal and priestly functions involving our care for one another. And it is based on our identity as stewards, responsible for all of creation. God told Adam to rule over and preserve every seed-bearing plant and tree, all birds of the air and fish of the sea, and all creatures that move on the ground. As members of Adam's race we have inherited this tremendous responsibility. We have been given a very high status, and one that commands great respect, and the more we grasp the honour of this and effectively fulfil our God-given roles, the more we will become aware of our own true worth. And this sense of worth will be manifested in our lives.

Christians with low self-esteem often try to boost it by telling themselves that, as they are God's children and have been accorded a high status as kings, priests, and stewards of creation, it doesn't matter if they are ugly, stupid, worthless.... But this is not true self-esteem. When there is a true inner knowledge of who we are in God, a knowledge that has sunk deep into the soul and is not merely an intellectual acknowledgment of truth, then the effect spills over into the material world. We start to feel beautiful, we begin to appreciate the capabilities of our own minds, and we sense our own value: we see ourselves as God sees us.

A true awareness of God's perception of us

Self-esteem is the assurance of being of value to God. And God perceives us as being of tremendous value. God likens us to treasure buried in a field, or a pearl of great worth sought by a wealthy merchant. Such is our value that God gave everything he had in order to redeem us.

Self-esteem is also the assurance of being accepted and approved by God. We are God's workmanship, his creation that he perceives as inherently good; a creator always loves and is proud of a well-made creation. Our respect for ourselves is increased when we also grasp the wonderful truth that, even though we have become broken and tarnished, through Christ we are being restored to our original glory:

> Once you were alienated from God and were enemies in your minds because of your evil behaviour. But now he has reconciled you by Christ's physical body through death to present you holy in his sight, without blemish and free from accusation — if you continue in your faith, established and firm, not moved from the hope held out in the gospel. [5]

Finally, self-esteem is the assurance of being lovable and loved. God made us in his image, which means, among other things, that we were made to be loved, and to pour out our love to others. Our being accepted as God's children, in spite of our shortcomings, demonstrates this. "How great is the love the Father has lavished on us, that we should be called children of God!" [6]

Being lovable and loved includes loving ourselves. Jesus said that the second greatest commandment is, "Love your neighbour as yourself".[7] It should be noted that we are told to love our neighbour *as* ourself — not instead of or better than ourself. We cannot truly love others until we have learned to love ourselves first. On this basis, 1 Corinthians 13 takes on a new meaning. Ask yourself:

> How patient are you with yourself?
> How kind are you to yourself?
> Do you easily get angry with yourself?
> Do you protect yourself?
> Can you trust yourself?

If you didn't score highly on the above, don't despair. Learning to love ourselves, like learning to esteem ourselves, is a life-long task; and a particularly difficult one. This is, in part, because people with low self-esteem are inclined to tell themselves that they should ignore their own needs and put everyone else first, so they end up fighting themselves. If this is you, then you may not even know what your own needs are, or even who you are. So you have a long way to go. Again, be patient with yourself, and remind yourself that wanting to improve your self-esteem is an indication that part of you *is* able to love yourself in a healthy way.

If you have been severely traumatised in the past, for example through having been abused, you may need help from a professional counsellor or psychotherapist. Abuse of any kind gives a subliminal message that you are merely there to be used, that your feelings don't count. Therefore, you will probably find it especially hard to believe that you are lovable, even if you have been able to believe that you are valuable, accepted, approved and loved. You can start developing this belief by telling yourself, over and over, that you *are* lovable, and that this is a biblical truth. This last is important because there is likely to be a little voice in your head telling you that you are deceiving yourself. This is the voice of people who have hurt you in the past, and it is the voice that is deceitful.

Also, keep reminding yourself that God intends you to esteem yourself because of who you are in him; that is, on the basis of a deep inner knowledge of a self that was created in God's own image and for whom Christ died. Knowing who you are in God does not give rise to false pride; one that merely disguises a low self-esteem. On the contrary, such knowledge is awe-inspiring — and very humbling. It is the foundation on which true self-esteem is built.

SUMMARY

The Christian message is a message of love. Many people come to God in the first place because, having low self-esteem, they feel unlovable and unloved, and they want to experience love. Becoming a Christian does not instantly resolve self-esteem problems; rather it means that there is a change of status, a change of disposition, and a change of direction. As self-esteem problems have usually arisen in childhood, through home or school circumstances, or the effects of exposure to societal standards and values, it can take a long time for the old patterns of self-devaluation to change. This is because the patterns lead to distorted views of the self, others and God, which affect attitudes and behaviour as adults. And the end results — lack of friends, broken marriages and poor functioning in the workplace — lower self-esteem even further.

Healthy self-esteem means that we don't have to hide from God, others or ourselves, and it is based on our identity in God. We are his children through creation and redemption, kings and priests, and stewards of the entire created world. Healthy self-esteem is also based on God's perception of us as essentially good, valuable, approved, accepted, lovable and loved. God wants us to grow and develop into well-rounded, healthy individuals who are able to relate to him and others without hindrance or fear. In order to do this, we begin by rejecting false guilt and others' false perceptions of us, and by clearing away misunderstandings about self-esteem. Then we need to start the process of opening up to God's love and, through his love, learn to love ourselves. This is the way of humility.

2

Self-identity — our existence in God

SHAPED AND FORMED BY GOD

Who we are: introduction

A strong sense of identity is the foundation on which self-esteem is built. We have to know ourselves before we can esteem ourselves. This includes knowing how we have been shaped and formed by God, who we are in God, and where we have been placed in the whole scheme of creation. We also need to know how we have been moulded by our national and religious history, by our culture, by our families, and by our own personalities.

In this chapter, the focus will be on our identity in God and creation. There will be some reference to our personal identity: how we have been shaped by events and trends in the past and by the society in which we now live. But this will be enlarged on in Chapter 3. We will commence by looking at different aspects of the self.

Who we are: the composition of the self

When God formed human beings, he made each of us an integrated whole, but with different parts: heart, mind, body, soul and spirit. For example, Jesus said, "Love the Lord your God with all your heart and with all your soul and with all your mind." [1] And Paul wrote, "May your whole spirit, soul and body be kept blameless at the coming of our Lord Jesus Christ." [2] For a healthy self-esteem, we have to feel positive about every aspect of the self. And we cannot do that until we have developed an awareness of every aspect, and have some idea of what the different parts consist of.

HEART

The Old Testament Hebrew words for heart, and the Greek New Testament word "kardia", refer to the governing centre of man's entire being; physical, emotional and intellectual. One of the Hebrew words, "nepes", is interchangeable with the Greek word for soul and indicates also the source of emotions or moral actions. In addition, "nepes" can mean "possessing life". In this respect it applies also to animals.

MIND

The two Hebrew words for heart are sometimes translated "mind"; while in the New Testament, there are several specific words for "mind". These refer to different aspects of reflective consciousness: perception, understanding, judging, meditating, and the formation of ideas and opinions. Bearing in mind that there is an overlap, for the purposes of this book the word "heart" will be used to denote the emotional part of a human that is especially concerned with love; "mind" will refer to the rational, thinking part.

BODY

In both the Old and New Testaments, the words translated "body" refer to the physical part of man — or to man's lower nature. But the physical body is not viewed merely as an outer case in which to house the soul. The Greek word "soma" especially indicates that the body is an integral part of man's entire being.

SOUL AND SPIRIT

The Greek words for soul and spirit, "psyche" and "pneuma", are also used interchangeably and may be translated as "life", although more often they refer to the emotions or desires, or to man's higher nature as a whole. The word "pneuma" (spirit) is comparable with the Hebrew "ruah", meaning "wind" or "breath", and refers also to that part of man which tends him towards God and enables him to commune with God: "The Spirit himself testifies with our spirit that we are God's children." [3] For the sake of consistency, the word "soul" will be used throughout

23

this book to refer to the sensing, feeling self, and "spirit" to the religious, God-seeking self.

Since man is an integrated whole and cannot be neatly divided into five distinct parts, it follows that low self-esteem in one area will adversely affect all the other areas. This is made clear in Scripture. The whole man has his origin in God, the whole man is tainted by sin, the whole man is redeemed, and the whole man will be taken up into heaven at the resurrection; although our natural bodies will be changed into spiritual ones. Similarly, because we are an integrated whole, we cannot boost self-esteem by focusing on only one aspect of the self.

There is a general tendency nowadays to work at enhancing self-esteem through learning how to make friends, get on in business, and improve physical appearance. These are all helpful, but they are not enough. For a true sense of inner worth we cannot afford to neglect the soul and spirit. The opposite also is true. Maybe you are a committed Christian, devoted to

God, working hard to be Christ-like, but you still feel bad about yourself. And maybe you have been told by well-meaning Christians that if only you trusted God more you wouldn't feel like that. But it is possible that the problem lies, not so much in your lack of spirituality, but in your neglect of the other areas: heart, mind and body. Or it lies perhaps in your neglect of the deepest levels of the soul: the essential self.

Who we are: the essential self

That part of man which we term "soul" is the most difficult to understand because basically it is intangible. And in this materialistic world, tangibles tend to be denied or overlooked. The soul is, in part, concerned with sensations and feelings, which can be grasped and understood. But ultimately, the soul, or psyche, is indefinable. It is what we really are: the essential self. And it is here, at the deepest levels, that the psychological and spiritual merge.

Although the essential self is intangible and indefinable, we can know the unknowable — just as we can know (experience) the love of God which passes (rational) knowledge, and which is at the core of our souls. It is only when we truly know, accept and love ourselves, living in complete harmony with ourselves, that we can experience the state of rest that God intended; a rest that is not shattered when the things that define us externally, such as our occupation, are removed. The search for self, and the God in us, is a life-long work; there is always more to discover, more heights to attain, more depths to plumb. And, as with the realisation of who we are in God, the more we know about ourselves, the more we realise that we don't know — and the more humble we become. The search for self must be guided by humility.

In a sense, everyone's soul is identical, so "finding ourselves" also puts us in touch with others. But at the same time, we are all different. The Celtic Christians thought of each individual soul as having a different shape, and it was considered important for each person to find his own unique shape. For a healthy self-esteem, you must not only know yourself, but also be yourself.

Perhaps you feel that you have been pushed, against your inclinations, into someone else's mould, that you don't know who you really are, or that you are out of touch with your true inner self. If any of these apply, then ponder how you may have been shaped by your upbringing, and identify those parts of you that don't feel right. Statements like, "This isn't really me", or "I don't feel myself today", can be very revealing. At the same time, consider those aspects of yourself that are more easily defined, being based on external factors.

Who we are: the visible self

Our personal identity is also founded on material factors, such as our roots. These include our national and cultural roots and our ecclesiastical roots: the way we think, feel and behave is influenced by what has gone before. But our individual make-up comes primarily from our own family.

We are also very much influenced by the culture and society in which we live. In this day and age a great deal of emphasis is placed on academic success. So we tend to define ourselves, and esteem ourselves, according to the position we hold in the workplace. In reality, however, our identity is based as much on our relational roles — who we are in relation to others, such as grandmother, stepfather, daughter-in-law — as on our occupational roles.

Our personal identity is also based on our characteristics, beliefs, moral standards, and values — what is important to us — and on our interests, likes and dislikes, and goals: what we would like to achieve and the kind of person we would like to become. We are our past, our present, and our future.

If you don't know where you belong, what roles you play in life, or what your beliefs, values and interests are, then think about yourself in the context of your country, church and family. Reflect on the jobs you have had and your current occupation, and consider your hobbies and interests, and how you feel about them. It might help you to write them down. All aspects of the visible self will be discussed more fully in the next chapter: our existence in time. However, of more importance is to discover your existence in relation to eternity.

OUR POSITION IN GOD

Made in his image

Imagine how the following beliefs would affect your self-esteem: we happened by chance, evolving through millennia from a blob of protoplasm. Or, man is a complicated machine. Like a clock, God made us, wound us up, and left us to our own devices. Now consider the truth: "In the beginning God created...." [4] We are here because God intended us to be here. And we were not mass-produced, all being turned out exactly the same. Neither were we left to fend for ourselves. Through Christ, God continues to uphold and sustain all of creation. "He [Christ] is the image of the invisible God, the firstborn over all creation. For by him all things were created.... He is before all things, and in him all things hold together." [5]

Perhaps the greatest wonder is that God created man in his own image. What this means cannot be said with any certainty, although it is generally accepted that man, like God, is made with the ability to think, feel and create. We are not made in God's physical image: "God is spirit, and his worshippers must worship in spirit and in truth." [6]

When God created man in his own image, he made him special, in part because of what he is: man alone is a spiritual being, able to commune with God's Spirit. Man is also special because of what he does. Man alone has concern about, and responsibility for, the rest of creation. We are commanded and equipped to exercise dominion. This does not mean dictatorship, but management, or stewardship.

When people have low self-esteem, there is a tendency to think, I'm a mistake, I shouldn't have been born. Or, I'm a waste of space; I don't serve any useful purpose. Have these thoughts ever crossed *your* mind? If so, then know that they are lies and must be refuted. God made you, he intended you to be here, and he has a special purpose for you. You must keep reminding yourself of this until the truth sinks deep into your soul and you start respecting and valuing yourself as God intended. At the same time, don't let any voices from the past tell you that you are bad and that you will never amount to anything. This too is a lie, and must also be challenged.

Perceived to be good

God saw that all of creation was very good. This seeing was a recognition and response to creation's inherent goodness, a goodness which has not essentially changed. The Fall did not destroy the image of God within; the spiritual nature remained. But the "flesh", or man's "lower nature", became dominant, and the higher, spiritual and intellectual powers of man were degraded; an effect which extended to the rest of creation. (Adam had a "lower nature" because he was less than God; the creation is always less than the creator.)

Because of Adam, we are born with a propensity to sin; a propensity that always leads to actual sin, so no man can attain the purity of God. We all fall short of God's glory. (We do not, as Pelagius taught, have the ability to attain God's righteousness through our own effort. But neither, as Augustine of Hippo and Calvin taught, are we a seething mass of sin with no real goodness.) What Christ did, through his sacrifice on the cross, was reverse the effects of the Fall. Through him the spiritual nature once again becomes dominant and we become, in effect, a new creation.

Like a masterpiece in art that had become lost beneath centuries of grime, dust and added paint, our worth lies in whose creation we are — for example, I am a Rembrandt — not primarily in what we are or how we appear to an undiscriminating world. Beneath the grime and dirt of sin and the amateur daubs of our own ignorance and shortcomings is the work of a master craftsman. And through Christ, the original is not just being restored to its former glory, it is being made anew.

People with low self-esteem tend to focus on their own faults and failings, and usually find it difficult to forgive themselves. But if Christ has forgiven us, what right do we have to condemn? True remorse, repentance and the ability to let go of the past and move on, which is the essence of forgiveness, come from God. But a harsh, judgmental attitude towards oneself, and a tendency to demand a superior, super-human perfection of oneself, is actually selfish, the opposite of healthy self-esteem. If this is your problem, then ask God to help you see beyond yourself and recognise the masterpiece within. When you are able to do this, you will also become increasingly aware of your relationship with God, and you will be able to appropriate and develop this in an atmosphere of trust and love — not in fear of condemnation.

OUR RELATIONSHIP TO GOD

We are God's children

We are God's children through creation. We were conceived in God's mind. "He chose to give us birth through the word of truth, that we might be a kind of firstfruits of all he created." [7]

And, we are God's children through redemption. "You are all sons of God through faith in Christ Jesus...." [8] Christ's sacrifice for sin makes us doubly God's children: we are his natural children and his adopted children, although the adoption will not be finalised until Christ's return in glory: "We ourselves, who have the firstfruits of the Spirit, groan inwardly as we wait eagerly for our adoption as sons, the redemption of our bodies." [9]

At the time of Jesus, those adopted were not babies or small children, but young men who were chosen by wealthy, childless couples because they were considered worthy to bear the family name and inherit the family wealth. As God's natural children — to whom he gave life — we have the sense of family identity. As God's adopted children, we have the sense of being chosen. Imagine how you would feel about yourself if your parents knew you before you were conceived and chose to have you because they esteemed you so highly. This is how it is with God.

We are kings and priests

Besides being children and heirs of God, we are "...a chosen people, a royal priesthood, a holy nation, a people belonging to God...." [10] Because Israel, God's original chosen people, rejected Christ, Christian believers become the new Israel, with all the rights and privileges, as well as the responsibilities, that this entails. We are also a royal priesthood. In the Old Testament, a king could not be a priest. But in Christ we acquire not only a royal status but also a priestly function, which we carry out whenever we pray for someone else. Furthermore, we are a holy nation. Holy means "set apart" and originally denoted the covenant (binding agreement) relationship between God and Israel. Through his sacrificial death, Christ became the mediator of a new covenant, one that we remember every time we celebrate the Lord's Supper.

Our relationship to God, as children, kings and priests, chosen and holy, indicates that we are of tremendous value to God; of great worth and deserving of very high esteem. But knowing this in our heads is not enough. The knowledge has to sink deep into our souls. You can initiate this process by focusing on the wonderful fact that you were both conceived and chosen by God, and by keeping on reminding yourself that you were meant to be here and that you have a very special responsibility, not only towards other people, but towards the entire created world.

OUR PLACE IN CREATION

Some misconceptions about creation

Over the centuries, some misconceptions about creation (nature) and our place in it have entered Christian thought. And some of these misconceptions are still prevalent today. Maybe you have accepted some of these beliefs, without really thinking then through. But it is important to consider them because false beliefs hinder the development of the true self.

Plato, a Greek philosopher, considered nature to be an impediment to the soul, which he perceived as being entombed in the body. He believed that it was man's task to bring order to nature and transcend it. Augustine of Hippo (AD 354-430) was one of those responsible for bringing Platonic ideas into the Christian Church, in particular the belief that all matter is evil and that emphasis should be placed on the spiritual. These beliefs can have major repercussions on how we perceive our own bodies.

Aristotle, a pupil of Plato, believed that nature was intrinsically ordered and that everything had a purpose, which was centred upon man: nature was there to be used. His views influenced medieval Christians who tended to despise nature. They had a fixed hierarchy of all created beings: the Great Chain of Being. Angels had the highest place in the chain. Then came man, who was considered the master of the earth. At the bottom of the chain was the world of insects. This view, in turn, influenced Victorian Christians: "The rich man in his castle, the poor man at his gate."

Today, Christians in general have reacted against this static view of society by emphasising that God wants us to experience material wealth and upward mobility. This is in part through the influence of Calvinist Protestants, who used nature in the belief that the elect are called to work and frugality, and that God would materially bless the chosen. The result is a tendency to think that, if we are struggling financially, or we are not getting our fair share of this world's goods, then God must be displeased with us, and we then feel even worse about ourselves.

Modern science, usually thought of as that developing in the 16th and 17th centuries, as exemplified by Newton and

Descartes, brought a mechanistic view of nature into the Christian Church. It was believed that God, a master mathematician, had caused the universe to run like clockwork. In this view, God no longer played a part in the world he had created. The Romantic view, which was a reaction against the mechanistic view, brought into Christian belief a focus on sensory experience and emotions. Nature was valued, not so much for its intrinsic, but for its aesthetic worth. This one-sided view is still pervasive today, and it affects not only how we perceive nature, but also how we perceive ourselves.

The Gaia hypothesis — a significant aspect of some of today's New Age movements — worships nature, which is associated with divinity. (Gaia is an old name for nature, mother, earth goddess.) In reaction to this pantheistic belief, the Christian Church of today has tended to give the environment scant attention, or even to ignore it, considering it to be relatively unimportant. And this keeps us from carrying out our God-given task.

There were, of course, exceptions in history. The early Church Fathers, for instance, believed in the redemption of all creation. And the Celtic Christians had a deep affinity with the entire created world, being aware of its inherent goodness and beauty, and of God's hand in everything. Exceptions in medieval times included the Franciscans — followers of St. Francis — and members of the Cistercian and Benedictine monasteries. They considered all creatures to be their brothers and sisters. Today, the concept of nature included in salvation is still strong in the Eastern Orthodox Church.

Here in the West there is, thankfully, an increasing awareness of the environment and our responsibility towards it. This knowledge is essential for our sense of integrity; misconceptions about creation are damaging to self-esteem.

The effects of misconceptions about creation

In addition to the effects already mentioned, the belief that man is no different from the animals leads to feelings of worthlessness, and a lack of true awareness and appreciation of the beauty and goodness of nature — including our own natures.

The belief that man is superior to the rest of creation, and can do what he likes with it, damages our integrity and leads to a general sense of alienation; a feeling of not being connected to anyone or anything. So, while it might be expected that this superior stance would boost self-esteem, it actually has the opposite effect.

The belief that man should worship nature distorts our perception of God and damages our relationship with him, and ultimately with all of creation. And any damaged relationship — especially with God — damages self-esteem.

Perhaps you have never considered your place in creation, or maybe you have thought that environmental issues were not the Church's responsibility. If you live in a city you may have little contact with nature and tend to forget its existence. But in order to have a true sense of yourself as God created you, it is important that you consider these issues, starting with Scripture.

Biblical teaching about creation and man's place in it

Man is a part of creation. He is made from the earth (adamah) as is everything else. Man shared a day of creation with the animals. But God created man higher than the animals, and he gave man responsibility for the care and protection of all created beings.

> You made him [man] a little lower than
> the heavenly beings and crowned him
> with glory and honour. You made him
> ruler over the works of your hands; you
> put everything under his feet: all flocks
> and herds, and the beasts of the field, the
> birds of the air, and the fish of the sea, all
> that swim the paths of the seas.[11]

To rule over creation, or have dominion over it, does not mean to use it indiscriminately for our own ends. We do not own creation, and we cannot do what we like with it. "The earth is the LORD's, and everything in it...." [12] We are merely tenants on the earth.

Taking responsibility and caring for creation are ways of

33

esteeming it; although, like us humans, all of creation has been affected by the Fall. "Cursed is the ground because of you; through painful toil you will eat of it all the days of your life." [13] The earth, which is an extension of self, was cursed because of man's inability to be in harmony with it.

> Hear the word of the LORD, you Israelites,
> because the LORD has a charge to bring
> against you who live in the land: "There is
> no faithfulness, no love, no acknowledgment
> of God in the land.... Because of this the
> land mourns, and all who live in it waste
> away; the beasts of the field and the birds of
> the air and the fish of the sea are dying." [14]

However, when Christ died, he died not just for humans, but for all of creation. "For God so loved the world...." [15] The word "world" is the Greek "kosmos", which can refer just to the human race, but actually means "the universe". Through Christ, creation itself will be "...liberated from its bondage to decay and brought into the glorious freedom of the children of God." [16] When Christ returns, there will again be harmony between man and the environment; a harmony in which, "The wolf and the lamb will feed together, and the lion will eat straw like the ox...." [17]

Perhaps you have thought that, in order to improve self-esteem you just have to learn how to make friends, influence people, be assertive, take charge.... These are all important, but the task is actually much greater. You have to learn how to be friends with all of creation, how to influence all of creation for good, and how to be assertive and take charge of all creation. This includes the animal world, the plant world, and everything God has made, in earth, sea and sky.

People with low self-esteem, who cannot relate to other people, are sometimes able to form a bond with animals. This is in part because animals accept us just as we are. They don't judge and condemn, they are responsive, and they give so much love. If this is how you are, then use your love of animals as a basis for

34

learning how to love people, including yourself. If you are not an animal or nature lover, start opening your eyes to the beauty around you, and thank God for his creation. This will enlarge your soul and motivate you to start doing more to help the environment. As you do so, you will find yourself developing a rapport with nature and a deeper respect for it, which in turn will lead to a deeper respect for yourself.

SUMMARY

Our self-esteem is based on our self-identity. We need to know who we are before we can truly love and esteem ourselves. God made man in his own image, with a heart, mind, body, soul and spirit, although these are not separate, clearly defined parts. Man is an integrated whole. At the deepest levels, each person's soul, which has its own unique shape, is integral with the spiritual self; with our existence in God. And, like God, the human soul can only be known experimentally — not factually. Our identity is also based on our socio-political, cultural, ecclesiastical and family history, on our relationships and the roles we play in life, and on our personal beliefs, values, interests and goals.

Of primary importance is our place in God and creation. We were made, and have remained, essentially good and beautiful, and of great intrinsic worth. And through Christ we have been accepted into God's family, with all the various functions, rights and responsibilities that this entails. Moreover, as humans, we have been created with the high position of stewards over all creation, the "kosmos" which God continues to love and value. When we start to grasp the extent of the honour that God has bestowed on us, and the enormity of our importance to him, then, in a spirit of humble thankfulness, we will begin to truly esteem ourselves.

3

Self-identity — our existence in time

OUR PLACE IN HISTORY — SOCIAL AND POLITICAL

Why history is important

What has happened in the past, whether or not we are aware of it, has contributed to making us what we are. Our history, which is linked with language, has helped determine the way we perceive things, and assisted in forming our values, beliefs, ethics and moral behaviour, as well as our social behaviour. It follows, then, that increased knowledge of the past will lead to increased knowledge of ourselves. It is partly because of this that the Bible encourages us to consider the past: "Remember the days of old; consider the generations long past. Ask your father and he will tell you, your elders, and they will explain to you." [1]

There are many different aspects of history that have combined to shape our general character and outlook. First, we are products of our national socio-political and religious past. As Christians, especially, we are also products of our ecclesiastical past, because of how church history has shaped our understanding and application of biblical truths. And, we are products of our cultural past. This includes the shaping of our perceptions, values and beliefs through literature, art and music, as well as through myth, legend and folklore. Finally, we are products of our family's past, which includes our own personal memories.

When we lose our memories, we also lose our identity. This was the aim of Big Brother in George Orwell's *Nineteen Eighty-Four*, because people who have no sense of themselves are easy to control. Memories, good, bad and indifferent, all go to making us what we are; and if they are accepted, worked through, and incorporated into our psyche, they create strength of character, with a corresponding high self-esteem.

Our identity is also linked with the identity of those who share our personal memories, whether directly or indirectly. We are all part of someone else's story, and there are many people, past and present, who are part of ours. As you seek to discover your identity, ask yourself, what books have I read, what TV programmes have I watched, what people have I met who have influenced my thinking and made me what I am today? Then think about people — and events — in history, who may have helped shape your thinking, beginning with the question, what is history?

What constitutes history?

In the 20th century West, we tend to regard something as history only if it is factual, without stopping to consider whose facts. For instance, much of what is considered history was written by historians long after the events they recorded. And two groups of people, or two warring nations, will record the same historical events very differently. There is also a tendency to consider history — or any other subject, such as geography or biology — in isolation. But just as the soul of man cannot be understood without reference to the other parts, history cannot be understood without reference to other areas of knowledge.

The emphasis on factual truth, and the modern trend of isolating subjects for learning purposes, has led to a general acceptance of recorded history as true, and a rejection of myth as untrue. But asking if a myth is true is like asking if music is true. It is the wrong question. Myths, as well as legends and folklore, are certainly not factual, but they do reveal a lot of truth about people, and ultimately about ourselves. Therefore, they also need to be considered.

You don't have to be a historian to have some under-standing of how you have been shaped by history — although maybe this chapter will whet your interest. The important thing is that you open your mind to different ways of perceiving. When self-esteem is low there is a tendency to be opinionated, to think

37

that there is only one way of looking at things. But as your self-esteem improves you will find that your mind becomes receptive to different facets of truth; and the more you are able to see from different perspectives, the greater will be your self-esteem. It is an upward-moving spiral. To start the process, we will look at a few examples of socio-political and religious events in British history that have helped form our national character and identity.

Our national heritage: British history

Britain has had a very chequered history, with invasions and infiltration by the Romans, Vikings, Anglo-Saxons and Normans. The last time England was conquered was at the Battle of Hastings in 1066, when Anglo-Saxon (north European) identity and traditions were subordinated to Norman dominance. As a result of this battle, England became part of medieval Europe, opening her up to new ideas and attitudes. The subsequent thousand years of invincibility have contributed to a sense of national pride and general feeling of superiority.

Henry VIII's break with Rome and the Reformation in the 1530s resulted, among other things, in the end of direct European influence, with a new political and religious freedom and the rise of Protestantism. The defeat of the Spanish Armada in 1588 enabled Queen Elizabeth I to keep England Protestant; and the new awareness of naval strength led to the beginning of colonial expansion, resulting in a strengthening of national pride and the further development of a strong national identity.

During the Industrial Revolution (18th and 19th centuries), Britain was the first country to change from an agricultural to an industrial society, becoming the "Workshop of the World". The Empire provided cheap raw materials and a captive market for finished goods, increasing British wealth and sense of well-being. Then came World War 1 (1914-1918). Bloodletting occurred on an unprecedented scale, leading to physical exhaustion and social upheaval, and giving rise to "the lost generation". In World War 2 (1939-1945) victory was achieved at tremendous economic cost, and industry was worn out. So, while national pride was enhanced, the cheapening of life and the destruction of ancient landmarks led to demoralisation and a sense of alienation.

With the loss of Empire (1948-1975), there was a further decline of national self-esteem, which in part was due to the sense of purposelessness. As Dean Acheson said, "Britain has lost an empire and not yet found a role." And now, with the entry into Europe (1970-present), for the first time since Henry VIII, European influence is becoming a significant factor in everyday life. So there is a continuing erosion of national identity.

Britain, then, has sometimes been a part of Europe, and at other times isolated. This alternation has resulted in a unique blend of northern and southern attributes and contributed to the formation of the ambivalent British character; an odd mixture of pride and self-effacement, openness and reserve, vulnerability and stoicism: the British stiff upper lip.

Perhaps you have felt at times that you are two different people — or more — being pulled in opposite directions. For example, one part of you may be outgoing and confident, while another part would rather hide away at home; one part may be very rational and logical, and another part dreamy and imaginative. This is normal. We are all many-sided, whatever our nationality, and often two sides will contradict each other. It is only abnormal when one aspect of the self is denied, so cannot be integrated into the other parts; or when the two sides are completely separate, as in the classic Jekyll and Hyde personality.

As you ponder how you may have been formed by your national history, try also to identify the different parts of yourself. Answering the following questions will help get you started.

1. What is your nationality — or nationalities? How does dual nationality affect your sense of identity?
2. Do you or any of your ancestors come from another country? What does this tell you about yourself?
3. What is your national heritage — Celtic, Anglo-Saxon, non-European...? And how does this affect you?
4. If you don't know your nationality, are of mixed race, or have lived abroad for a long time, how does this affect your sense of self?

As we are affected, not only by our religio-political and social past, but also by our cultural heritage, we will now look at history from the perspective of myths, legends and folklore. Our cultural heritage also includes the history of art, literature and music, in all their various forms, which is too big a subject to include here; although, for a greater understanding of yourself, you may want to explore this aspect of history on your own.

OUR CULTURAL HERITAGE — MYTHS, LEGENDS AND FOLKLORE

Our Celtic past

For those with a Celtic heritage, primarily the Welsh, Irish and Scottish, the exploits of the ancient Celts and their deities, as told in *The Mabinogion*, are of major importance in explaining general attitudes and outlooks. Also of significance are the Celtic-Medieval legends of King Arthur, as told in Malory's *Le Morte d'Arthur*. Celtic myths and legends have contributed especially to a deep sense of the spiritual, and an appreciation and awareness of the natural world; and their impact is demonstrated in creative expression through music and poetry. Celtic myths and legends live on in such things as British place names, church decoration and folk customs.

Our Nordic past

The Icelandic (Viking) Eddas are a major source of information about our Nordic mythological past, which has also helped to create the British character, especially evident in northern pessimism, as in the story of Beowulf. We are also influenced by the stories of Germanic heroes and gods, described in the *Nibelungenlied*. The sense of "Götterdämmerung" ("the twilight of the gods"), or sense of impending doom, is derived from both Viking and Germanic mythology. All the best northern myths are tragic, with heroism as the only source of light and hope in the darkness and chaos.

Both Viking and Germanic myths and legends have also played a part in forming the English belief in his superiority. The

German hero, Siegfried, meaning "peace through victory", is the same as the Viking Sigurd. Viking and Germanic beliefs persist in customs and folklore, but particularly in our language. For example, the days of the week are named after Scandinavian deities.

Greek influence

Because Greek culture was widespread in the first centuries AD, Britain is to a large extent also shaped by Greek mythology, which is basically optimistic and far more sensual than the Northern and Celtic myths. The Greeks enjoyed, rather than feared, their gods, who were idealised men and women. And, rather than a place of twilight gloom, the Greek paradise was warm and welcoming. Evidence of Greek culture abounds in Britain, not only in literature, art and architecture, but also in the general British outlook.

Non-European influences

There are many Britons who are influenced, not by Nordic, Celtic and Greek mythology, but by the myths and legends of their countries of origin. It is impossible to mention all of them, but a general glance at the myths of Africa and India will provide some food for thought. In many African myths, which affect also Caribbean thinking and outlook, there is a closeness to nature. In this respect they share an affinity with Celtic myths. However, while all the indigenous British myths perceive the sun to be all-important, in many African myths it is the rain gods who are accorded the highest status.

In India, especially in Hinduism, rivers are seen as the source of support and spiritual life, and thinking is in terms of the flow of life, a person being moulded by his karma: thoughts and actions in a previous existence. The legends surrounding the prince Buddha (563-483 BC), have similarly given rise to an emphasis on a person's inner being, and placed a high value on the spiritual. The Buddhist attempt to achieve nirvana can be compared with the western psychological attempt to achieve actualisation; to realise one's full potential.

There is a close link between mythology and psychology: the area of the soul. So we cannot entirely ignore our mythological past if we truly want to know and understand ourselves. As with history, we needn't be experts on the subject. What is important is that we recognise that we do not exist in a vacuum, that our beliefs and values have been formed, not only by our country, religious heritage and personal past, but also by our distant past. In order to gain some appreciation of how you may have been shaped by your culture, answer the following:

1. What is your cultural heritage — Celtic, Nordic...?
2. If, like most Britons, your heritage is mixed, which one do you most identify with, and why?
3. Which of your beliefs and values do you think may be, in part, products of your cultural past?
4. How do you think a mythological past that focused on the sun would make your general outlook different to that of someone whose mythological past emphasised the importance of rain or rivers?

42

Mythology is not only closely akin to psychology, but also to religion. And for believers who are citizens of a country that, for hundreds of years, has been Christian, our ecclesiastical past is also of major importance.

OUR ECCLESIASTICAL PAST

The Church's foundation

The Church is described as a building made with living stones. It was built on the twelve apostles — who had their roots in Judaism — Jesus Christ himself being the chief cornerstone. Christians today are usually well informed about this apostolic age, and about the modern eras of Church history, with some knowledge of major events and reformations. But there is a general tendency to leave out whole chunks of our ecclesiastical heritage. Between us and the founding apostles a lot of building has been going on, which we ignore or reject at our peril. We need to know about Church history, its beliefs, customs and traditions, not only to learn from the past, but also to have a firmer sense of who we are.

Tradition

During this last century, some Christians have also tended to shy away from tradition, associating it with legalism, which Jesus condemned. He asked the Pharisees and teachers of the law, on more than one occasion, why they broke the commands of God for the sake of their tradition. And the apostle Paul wrote: "See to it that no-one takes you captive through hollow and deceptive philosophy, which depends on human tradition and the basic principles of the world rather than on Christ." [2] Tradition certainly can become burdensome, blocking the natural spontaneity and freedom that is essential for a healthy self-esteem. But to reject tradition itself is to lose our sense of belonging: we become isolated from other believers, past and present.

Tradition is defined as precepts or customs passed down from past generations. As Christians, our faith must be based on the precepts, or teachings, of Christ. But as well as developing our own traditions, we must also respect the customs of the past, and of other groups of Christians, as did Jesus and Paul. We are told that Jesus went into the synagogue as was his custom, and Paul did nothing to offend against the customs of the people or the ancestors. It is through traditions, such as reciting the Lord's Prayer or the Nicene Creed, that we retain our links with the past, and enhance our sense of self.

When self-esteem is low, there is a tendency to feel isolated, and even to expect rejection and exclusion. If you feel that you are a misfit in your local church, that you don't really belong, the problem could be that your damaged self-esteem is distorting your perception of others. But maybe the problem goes deeper and you have allowed yourself to become isolated from the Church universal. A glance at some of those influential Christians in history who tend to get overlooked, with reference to how they have affected current beliefs, will start the process of putting you back in touch. You are not alone in your struggles of faith, although at times it may seem like it.

Some influential church leaders and writers
The early apostolic fathers, such as Clement and Barnabas, were still trying to define their beliefs in the face of opposition and persecution. Their struggles, questions, doubts, and changing views and emphases ultimately led to their leaving a legacy of faith that we would do well to understand.

Tertullian (160-200), the first major Christian author to write in Latin rather than Greek, had very strict views on moral behaviour, and his influence is still felt in many sectors of the Christian Church today. His contemporary, Origen (c.184-254), who was also a great scholar, and a prolific writer, expressed his beliefs in Platonic terms. Much of what we tend to think of as Christian is in fact the teachings of Plato.

Athanasius (c. 296-373), important because of his part in defining the Trinity, did much to promote monasticism, with all that this entailed. And Augustine (354-430) was instrumental in recognising and teaching that salvation is a free gift, although he too brought Platonic ideas into the Christian Church.

The medieval theologian and writer, Thomas Aquinas (1225-1274), tried to synthesise Aristotelian philosophy with Christian teaching, again with lasting effect. And the German monk, Thomas à Kempis (c. 1380-1471), a forerunner of Martin Luther, wrote the very influential devotional book, *The Imitation of Christ*, which is still a bestseller. Thomas Cranmer (1489-1556), who was martyred for his faith, is important because of his role in formulating the articles of the Church of England.

There are many, many more — people like the above, as well as more famous figures like Luther, Calvin, Jonathan Edwards and the Wesley brothers — to whom we owe a great debt for their part in defining our faith and directing our thinking and behaviour. And in addition to the great catalogue of influential people, there are also many significant events or eras in Church history that have helped form our identity.

Some significant events and eras in Church history

The apostolic age of the New Testament was followed by the persecution era, the evolution of the Roman Church, Celtic Christianity and medieval mysticism, all of which played a part in shaping our beliefs and general outlook and attitudes. A major change occurred with the Lutheran Reformation (1517) and the Protestant Cause, which was largely brought about through Calvin, who was converted in 1533.

In our own country, Wyclif's (c.1329-1384) translation of the Bible into English had tremendous spiritual and psychological impact, as did the break with Rome and the Reformation in England, and the Wesleyan revival (18th century). Other events, both positive and negative, include Darwin's very influential book, *On the Origin of Species* (1859), and the mechanistic view of "God as clockmaker", both of which challenged and modified Victorian Christian thinking. Then came the Welsh revival of 1904 and the Pentecostal revival, the Jesus generation, the 20th century emphasis on the individual....

We are part of a great and wonderful Church. And knowing this, and something of the Church, gives us a firm sense of who we are and where we belong. We need to be acquainted with those who went before, and understand how they tried to apply biblical truths to their own times and lives. The tendency nowadays to focus on the apostolic and modern eras leaves a 2,000-year gap. Filling the gap in our ecclesiastical past also fills a gap in our own psyche.

You can fill your own gap by opening yourself up to new areas of knowledge, beginning where your interests and natural tendencies lie, and at the level you are most comfortable with. There are many good books on different aspects of Church history, and biographies of influential leaders. But maybe a good starting point would be to read about or talk to people of your own era. There are probably many elderly people in your church who would love to tell you about their younger days as a Christian. At the same time, you can also increase your knowledge of your own family.

OUR PERSONAL MAKE-UP

Who we are: our family history

The more you know about your family, the firmer will be your sense of personal identity. It can help if you not only know about your parents and grandparents, but something of your family tree. But it may be that you are unable to trace your family of origin, perhaps through having been adopted. Or you may be ashamed of your family and not want to get involved with it. In either case, a firm sense of who you are in God will enable you to rise above any feelings of lostness and isolation. "Though my father and mother forsake me, the LORD will receive me." [3]

However, knowing that you are part of God's family, and that he will provide you with surrogate human families, does not mean that you can dismiss your own family as unimportant. Your family matters. And if their influence has been negative, it is essential that you acknowledge this to yourself, work through the pain of rejection or abuse, and ultimately forgive. This will enhance your sense of self, whereas by denying your family you will also be denying a part of yourself. Included in your family history is the name your parents chose for you.

Who we are: our names

A name reflects an era, geographical location, our parents' preferences, expectations.... Nowadays, parents often choose names for their children simply because they like the sound of them. Or, they may name a child after a relative, a film or sports star, or a place.

In Bible times, names had great significance. They reflected character or described God's current dealings with Israel. For instance, Adam gave his wife the name Eve, which means "life giver", and Lamech called his son Noah, meaning "comfort". Joseph was told to call Mary's son Jesus (Hebrew Y'shua), meaning "salvation", because he would save his people from their sins. His name indicated that he was the promised holy one of Israel. Old Simeon in the temple recognised this, and said, "...my eyes have seen your salvation...." [4] that is, "your Y'shua".

How did Jesus feel about his name? And how did it affect his self-esteem? In Greek it was Iesous, in Hebrew Y'shua, a variant of Yesha-Yahu, "God saves". In the Jewish Talmuds he was known as Y'shua Ben Pandera, which is a term of insult. It possibly means Jesus son of no-one, or Jesus the bastard.

How do you think God feels about your name? And how do you feel about it? Whatever your views, your name is important to God. He calls us by name. Our names are written in heaven. And there we will have a new name, reflecting what we have become on our journey through life; that is, our fully developed identity. If you were to choose a new name for yourself, what would you choose, and why? And how would it reflect your sense of self, and describe your attributes?

Who we are: our attributes

Our attributes are traits or characteristics that are consistent over time. They may be positive, for example, "I am gentle and kind." Or they may be negative: "I have a cruel streak." In Britain especially, there is a reticence about blowing one's own trumpet. And few people like admitting to their less attractive qualities. But humbly acknowledging your own God-like attributes is necessary for a true sense of identity. It is also essential that you admit your shadow side. Being a Christian means being in the process of changing into his likeness, so the light side of self becomes progressively brighter and the shadow part recedes. Those attributes that define us may be relatively stable, but they are not fixed — unlike our gender.

Who we are: our gender

Apart from inborn traits that make boys different from girls, the two sexes are brought up differently. Gender confusion — the feeling that we were born into the wrong body — or confusion about sexual orientation, erodes self-esteem, because a strong sense of one's gender, and a liking for and appreciation of one's gender, is essential for a healthy view of oneself.

Do you like being the gender God made you? Are you comfortable with your body? If you have problems in this area, then begin resolving them by reminding yourself that God created male and female, and that he made men and women equal but with different, very important roles and functions. We are meant to complement each other and to esteem each other. If you are unable to accept your gender, or have unresolved problems with sexual orientation, you may need professional help to overcome your difficulties in this area. Unresolved gender problems erode every area of life, and especially affect relationships.

Who we are: our roles

Roles may be relational, such as father, mother, daughter, nephew. Or they may be occupational: secretary, doctor, builder.... In this day and age there is a tendency to judge people by their occupational roles — or lack of them. And the vital role of mother especially is downgraded. Academic roles are generally valued more than technical skills, although in the Bible those who could work with their hands were accorded high status. It is easy for Christians to get caught up in the world's values and to feel worthless and undervalued as a result. Recognising the great worth God places on human relationships, especially that of mother, and the value he accords to all human talents and abilities, is essential for a strong sense of identity.

What roles do you play in life, and how much value do you place on each? Have you been unduly pressured by today's society? Asking yourself these questions is the first step towards developing that part of your identity which is based on relational and occupational roles, and discovering your beliefs and values.

Who we are: our beliefs and values

Do you know what you believe and why? What we believe helps to define us as individuals. Also of importance is how we believe. Do you have firm beliefs that are open to question and change, or do you rigidly hold onto your beliefs, afraid to consider anything different? Are you tossed by every wind of doctrine? Identity is not static; it is constantly changing. And in order to retain a healthy sense of self we need, like the early Church fathers, to periodically reassess, and either reaffirm or modify our beliefs.

49

Our values are what is important to us. We may, for instance, believe that Bible reading is necessary for Christian growth, but not attach too much importance to it. Or we may believe in something so passionately — such as conservation — that we devote our lives to it. Have you ever stopped to consider what your values are, and why? Values often change with altered circumstances, or with age. In order to be sure about yourself, you need to know what is important to you now. And it is essential to periodically question those values that have remained static over a long period of time. The stasis may indicate a firm sense of who you are in God or, conversely, that you have stopped growing. Another possibility is that past interests have waned without being replaced, and there is no longer any sense of direction.

Who we are: our interests and goals

What we like to do, or hate doing, says a lot about us. Our interests help define us as individuals, and lack of them not only indicates stifled curiosity — see Chapter 5 — but also a poor sense of identity. Do you know what your interests are? Do you have hobbies? Do you know what your particular dislikes are? If you want to know yourself, you must know what things attract and engage you, and why. Like beliefs and values, our interests, likes and dislikes change over time.

We are also defined by our hopes and ambitions. Our identity is based, not only on what we are, but also on what we hope to be, and on what we would like to achieve. Our future plans are linked with current interests and values, and are an indication of personal growth and development. What do you hope for in life? Do you have goals? What steps are you taking to reach those goals? For a firm sense of identity, you must know where you are going. Remember, we are our future, as well as our past and present.

It is not just the different aspects of our past and present, and future hopes and dreams, that have contributed to forming our identity, but the interplay between them. For instance, what we have experienced in the past influences current beliefs and values, and these in turn determine future choices. At the same time, our present state of mind affects our perception of the past, leading us to select, or reject, specific features, and these influence how and why we choose our future goals.

Because of this interplay, self-identity is not easy to pin down, in spite of there being some aspects of the self that can be recognised and labelled. However, a general awareness of who we are in God and through creation, and of how we have been shaped by history and our own families and personalities, will give a firmer base on which to develop the self. Therefore, before you go forward, growing in God and developing each of the different parts of self — heart, mind, body, soul and spirit — first look back, not in anger, but with humble gratitude for all the good things that have gone before.

SUMMARY

Our self-identity, who and what we are, is based not only on our place in God and creation, but also on our socio-political past which, in Britain, has contributed to the formation of the ambivalent British character. We are also products of our cultural past, which includes the history of art, music and literature, as well as myths, legends and folklore. And we are products of our ecclesiastical past. This covers two thousand years of Church history, with its struggles, doubts, questions, backslidings and reformations, and changing emphases.

Our identity also consists of our personal history and attributes: our name, gender, and our past and present relationships and roles, beliefs, values and interests, and our goals for the future. Identity is not static: we are what we have been, what we are now, and what we hope to become; and each affects the other. The stronger our sense of identity, the greater potential there is for developing a healthy self-esteem; it is the foundation on which self-esteem is built.

4

Self-esteem — the social self (heart)

A HEART MADE TO LOVE

The need for love

The heart is generally considered to be that part of man concerned with the receiving and giving of love. Love is man's greatest need, and when someone has been hurt during the childhood years, the need for love is especially strong. But the betrayal of trust that goes with pain and rejection makes it very difficult for such people to accept love, even when it is freely offered.

Hurt people also find it hard to give love. They tend to love exclusively, pouring out an intense, possessive ardour on just one other person, rather than loving everyone and everything as God intended. And their love is based on need. Their deepest concern is to make people love them, so they give in order to receive. Since hurt people cannot love openly and spontaneously, they cannot form healthy relationships, so they are hurt over and over again, with the result that low self-esteem is reduced even further.

We can only truly love as we experience love, beginning with the love of God; a love so vast and amazing that it passes human knowledge. As we receive love, we learn first to love ourselves, and then to love others. If you have difficulty with love, and find it hard to form healthy, lasting relationships, perhaps it is because you have been trying to give before you have received. You cannot give what you do not have. Perhaps also you have never been able to fully believe that God loves you unconditionally — just as you are. Maybe you don't even know what love is.

What is love?

Two Greek words in the New Testament describe the love of the Father for the Son, and for all believers. "Agapé" is an unselfish, sacrificial love, an act of the will, while the verb "phileo" describes a tender affection. The psychoanalyst, Erich Fromm, described love as having four basic elements, which are mutually interdependent: knowledge, respect, responsibility and care. As these accord with the biblical concept of love, we will define love by breaking it down into these four components.

First, love consists of knowledge, commencing with a knowledge of ourselves. We cannot know others if we have never got to know ourselves: who we really are inside. There are many layers of knowledge, and the deeper the love the deeper the knowledge, that is, the ability to see into the deepest reaches of the soul. When we love we are able to recognise another's essential self, and identify that person's true feelings, even if they are hidden or disguised. For example, overt anger may be hiding an inner fear; arrogance may be covering an underlying insecurity. But knowledge must be guided by respect and care. Fromm points out that the desire for knowledge without respect and care is the essence of sadism.

Respect is also part of love; the word comes from the Latin "respicere" — to look at. It is the ability to see a person as he is, to be aware of his unique individuality. It follows, then, that we can only truly know a person if we respect, that is, see properly. And since respect is also the concern that another should grow and develop as he is, for his own benefit, in his own way and in his own time, it must be based on knowledge. Respect and knowledge are built on each other, and they provide the foundation for responsibility and care. When we respect another's uniqueness, we will not be tempted to make comparisons, be impatient, exploit, be intrusive, or try to turn the other into a little replica of ourselves. Respect is associated with freedom, and allowing others to be free is possible only if we have achieved a certain independence regarding our own emotional needs.

Love also means being responsible for others. We *are* our brother's keeper. In its true sense responsibility is a voluntary act, not something carried out from a sense of duty. It is our response to another's needs, and it involves knowing what those needs are, and when and how to meet them in an acceptable way. It also requires that we be constantly in tune with the other's changing and fluctuating needs, which we can only do if we are first in tune with ourselves.

Finally, love is caring. Care means being concerned about another and wanting to help, so it is linked with responsibility. We are meant to look after each other's welfare, not because we feel we have to, but because we are genuinely interested in seeing that the other's physical, emotional and spiritual needs are met. Care also means being emotionally touched by another's griefs and joys, and in a sense sharing them as we reach out in empathy and understanding.

When we are able to give love that is based on knowledge, respect, responsibility and care, we make others feel safe and warm, and they naturally feel good about themselves; their self-esteem is enhanced. And as we make others happy, we also benefit ourselves. But, as has been said, we can only give love as we are able to experience love. Unless love is constantly flowing into us we will dry up and become a stagnant pool, with nothing left to give.

If you feel constantly drained, it could be that you are acting on the old adage, "Jesus first, others second, yourself last", driving yourself to give and give, and neglecting yourself in the process. It is not selfish to have your own emotional and spiritual needs met, any more than it is selfish to eat healthily and keep yourself warm and safe. It is essential. You have to be able to receive.

RECEIVING LOVE

Receiving love from God

The kind of love God has for us is sacrificial and giving; it includes a tender affection and consists of knowledge, respect, responsibility and care. God's love is unconditional; it does not vary and change as we do, sometimes living in step with God and at others stubbornly going our own way. He loves us because he made us, and because we are essentially good, valuable and lovable; he loves us because we are his children, his offspring, part of himself. When we come to understand this, to grasp the enormity and wonder of it, God's love becomes awe-inspiring, and so very humbling. And it is only when we are truly humbled, when we are able to put aside any false sense of being bad, worthless and unlovable that we can start receiving and appropriating God's love in all its fullness. It is arrogance and defiance that makes us reject God's love.

It is also arrogance that makes us think that we cannot be forgiven; that our sins are so much greater than anyone else's because more is demanded of us. And this feeling of having to be perfect in every respect, which is actually a sign of low self-esteem, makes it difficult to forgive ourselves, so there is a tendency to get stuck, emotionally and spiritually. There is an inability to move beyond our own, and others', failures and shortcomings. But Jesus said, "...he who has been forgiven little loves little." [1] The opposite also is true: the more we are able to receive God's love in the form of forgiveness, the more we will be able to forgive.

If you have difficulty believing that God loves you unconditionally, and you find it hard to feel forgiven and to forgive yourself, perhaps you should ask yourself what the problem is. Is it, in fact, a self-esteem one that has given you a distorted view of yourself; a view that seems like humility but is actually pride? If the answer is yes, then ask, and receive, God's forgiveness for your inability to feel forgiven. Then, learn how to accept love and forgiveness from others.

Receiving love from others

God intended us to be loved by our fellow men. He made us to love and be loved. But people with low self-esteem have problems receiving love because they feel so inadequate and undeserving. They tend therefore to be suspicious, so they cannot accept compliments or praise. They are likely also to be shy or withdrawn, and they may compensate for their own feeling of inadequacy by being critical and putting others down. All these actions are rejecting — the opposite of love. Being able to accept love graciously is, paradoxically, a way of expressing love.

Another reason why people with low self-esteem have difficulty receiving love is because they fear rejection. They tend, therefore, to reject others first. Or, they may put on a facade or suit of armour to keep others from getting too close. They might even physically avoid others. These actions too are very unloving, although they are usually not intended to be: they make others feel rejected or foolish, and deprive them of the joy of giving.

Without the ability to receive love, what we may think of as love may actually be need: we are nice to others because we need them to love us. Everyone, of course, performs kind acts for others with mixed motives. No one is purely altruistic. The important thing is to be aware of our own reasons for doing good. This is part of knowing ourselves, and it acts as a safeguard, preventing our unintentionally harming others through ignorance of what *they* really need.

In order to learn how to receive love, and so boost your self-esteem, begin by questioning your motives for helping others, especially if you are a very busy person, constantly dashing around looking after everyone else, or if you are in a caring profession. Then, work at putting aside any false sense of independence, while continuing to reject the lie that you are unlovable. It is only as you open up to love and become capable of accepting affection, compliments, praise, encouragement and practical help from others that you can grow and develop into the loving person you want to be, and that God wants you to be.

GIVING LOVE

Giving love to God

First, we must give love to God. We love him because he first loved us. Our love for God is initially based on need; it is only as we grow spiritually, becoming rooted and grounded in his love, that we are able to love him for what he is rather than for what he does for us. Job reached this place when he was able to trust God even if God were to slay him, thereby failing to meet his need for self-preservation. We must love God with all our heart, soul and mind. The love God demands for himself is "agapé" love.

Loving God means being willing to die for him. It means *wanting* to give to him, rather than giving out of a sense of fear or duty. Loving God means lavishly pouring out a warm and spontaneous devotion. It means praising and worshipping him, enjoying being with him. And it means obeying him. Jesus said, "If you love me, you will obey what I command." [2]

If you have difficulty loving God, perhaps it is because you don't know him. Remember, love consists of knowledge. Therefore, seek to know God through daily walking with him, talking to him and learning about him. And identify those areas where you have the most difficulty loving. For example, you may find it possible to obey, but not to be open and spontaneous. Then work at overcoming your particular difficulties, through recognising how the problems arose and finding constructive ways of supplying your lack in those specific areas. As your needs are met, you will be freed to love others.

Giving love to others

Jesus commanded us to love our neighbour as ourselves, and he enlarged our concept of "neighbour" through the story of the good Samaritan. According to this story, no one should be excluded from our love. Both "agapé" and "phileo" are used in the New Testament to describe the love we should have for others.

There are several categories of people included in the concept of "neighbour". First, God commands us to love and care for our families, not only for our spouses and children, but for any relative in want. We are also commanded to love our fellow believers. Love for our brothers and sisters in Christ is, in fact, the proof of discipleship. John, the disciple whom Jesus loved and who became the apostle of love, went so far as to say that if we do not love, then we do not know God. And we must love even when we are not loved in return. Finally, we must love even our enemies, those who are actively against us. This last is "agapé" love.

There are many different ways of showing love to our neighbour: through practical giving and helping, through meeting their emotional needs, and through encouraging and assisting spiritual growth. Making up for another's emotional deprivation, when the other has been brought up in a dysfunctional family setting, is especially pertinent. However, caution is needed here. People who have experienced abuse or rejection in their own lives tend to be attracted to others from similar backgrounds, and to want to make them feel better. This is in part a psychological need to vicariously meet our own needs through meeting others'. But when we are able to receive love, and therefore get our own needs met in a healthy, constructive way, we are able to love other damaged people as they need to be loved, without overburdening ourselves in the process.

Providing for another's emotional requirements, especially when they were not satisfied during their childhood, is a form of re-parenting, and it demonstrates the father/motherhood of God. Children — and damaged adults, who retain more of the child in them than the average grown-up — have five basic emotional needs. The first is to be nurtured, that is, built up through the provision of affirmation, support and empathy. Children also need to feel safe, to have firm and consistent boundaries and know that trust will not be betrayed. The third need is for loving and gentle discipline, which means guidance and direction, not punishment. Children also need an accepting environment that allows them the freedom to be spontaneous and open, and to have fun. Above all, children need to be shown affection, to be loved and accepted, just as they are.

These, to some extent, are also the needs of adults, however mature. So they are also your needs. And the more they are satisfied, the more you will be able to meet the needs of others; to love everyone, believer or unbeliever, friend or foe, and to love in a way that is consistent with *their* needs and that will boost *their* self-esteem. As you see others finding healing from past hurts, and blossoming and growing through the experience of your love, your self-esteem also will be boosted — and you will find it easier to love yourself. Loving ourselves enables us to love others, and loving others helps us to love ourselves.

Giving love to ourselves

When Jesus commanded us to love our neighbour *as*, or in the same way as, ourselves, it was a recognition that we cannot do for others what we are unable to do for ourselves. It was also a recognition that we cannot give something we haven't got: we have to receive in order to give. Love that is bailed out from a stagnant pool is unhealthy, unlike the love that flows from a pool that is constantly being replenished. And the more love flows in, the more it can flow out. Giving love to ourselves means that we know ourselves, respect ourselves, take responsibility for ourselves and care for ourselves.

Part of our responsibility for ourselves is to get our own needs met, especially if there has been an unhappy childhood. This might involve having counselling, which, with many theoretical models, is partly about meeting clients' emotional needs through re-parenting. Or there may be a motherly person in your church who wants someone to care for. When self-esteem has been damaged because of a parent's abuse, abandonment, rejection, alcoholism, or whatever, God very often brings about healing, not through one parental figure, but through a variety of people. So a surrogate parent might be a composite. For instance, one person might be very affectionate and meet that particular childhood requirement, while another is a good listener, and yet another enjoys helping out practically.

So, in order to love yourself, first work at recognising your own areas of emotional deprivation, and set about fulfilling your needs in a healthy, constructive way. And don't let feelings of worthlessness get in the way. Maybe you think that there is no one around to care for you. Or that people don't even talk to you, so how on earth are they going to provide for your emotional needs? If this is the case, your first step might be to learn all about friendship, and to start making friends.

FRIENDS AND FRIENDSHIP

Why we need friends

Growth and development, with the subsequent raising of self-esteem, occurs within the context of relationships. We need families, and when we don't have an earthly family, because of bereavement, geographical isolation or rejection, God ensures that we are not left alone. We also need friends. People who have been hurt tend to shut themselves away and avoid social situations, telling themselves that they don't need anyone. But this is emotional and spiritual suicide. In order to be emotionally healthy and spiritually mature, we need people.

The fact that we need people has been proved on several fronts. Anthropological studies have shown that humans cannot develop properly, physically or culturally, in isolation; while from a socio-psychological standpoint, it has been demonstrated that it is damaging to one's emotional and mental well-being to be cut off from others. And from the biblical point of view, God has said, right from the dawn of creation, it is not good for man to be alone.

Social isolation is a phenomenon that became more widespread and pervasive during the twentieth century. This is because of the changes from rural to urban living, from being stationary to mobile, and from being part of the local community to being part of the "global village". These changes have led to reduced self-esteem because of feelings of insignificance, just being one in a crowd; instability, through lack of roots and little or no sense of belonging; and impotence, the feeling of being just a small voice in a big world. Now, perhaps more than at any other time in history, we need friends.

What friendship is

The traditional view of friendship, based on Aristotle's understanding of it, has three essential components: friends must enjoy one another's company, friends must be useful to one another, and they must share a mutual commitment to that which is good and wholesome, bringing out the best in each other and thereby benefiting others. In Britain today, this last component is usually neglected and friends are made for unhealthy reasons; those arising from low self-esteem and leading to yet lower self-esteem.

People with self-esteem problems tend to be shy, lacking in confidence, and unable to be assertive: to express their views and feelings in constructive ways that do not belittle or damage others. Instead, they are likely to be either passive or, at the other extreme, aggressive. There is often hypersensitivity to perceived put-downs, an inability to handle criticism, and a propensity to attribute bad motives to others and be critical of others. All these lead to a tendency to make the wrong type of friends or to demand too much from them, putting a strain on the relationship, or to make friends for the wrong reasons.

A healthy person, on the other hand, has a wide circle of acquaintances, several friends with whom to share meals or outings, and a few close friends who can be confided in. It is unrealistic, and a symptom of damaged self-esteem, to expect all friendships to be on the same level.

Of course, it takes two to make a friendship, and if you are finding it difficult to make friends, perhaps through having just moved to a new area, it might not be because of anything lacking in you. But if you have a self-esteem problem, it would be well to question yourself. Do you tend to shy away from people? Are you able to make and keep friends? Do you have only one or two intense friendships that are all consuming? Do *you* seek friends for the wrong reasons?

Unhealthy reasons for having friends

When friends are acquired in order to boost a low self-image, those preferred are people of the same age and with the same interests; that is, friends who are most likely to be approving. Friends chosen are also likely to be those who flatter or hero-worship; those who are worse off, financially or morally, and who make you look good in comparison; and those who are less intelligent: friends whom you can instruct and teach, thereby making you feel superior. When there has been a history of abuse, there is an especial tendency, as has been mentioned, to gravitate towards people with dysfunctional family backgrounds, and part of the compulsion to help such people comes from an unconscious need to feel in control.

When friends are acquired in order to get ahead, for instance, in the business world, those preferred are people who can be manipulated and used; that is, people who can pull strings, or who can give you greater social standing, either through being your passport to an elite society or who are useful for name-dropping. Also preferred are friends who are hero-worshipped, so that you can bask in their reflected glory.

When friends are acquired to give life a meaning, those likely to be chosen are people who belong to a sub-culture, such as a neighbourhood gang or secret society, who can give you a sense of identity and purpose. There is also an inclination towards people who manipulate, and who thereby make you feel useful; friends in need, to whom you can devote your life; and friends with a cause, whom you can blindly follow.

If you have a tendency to make friends for unhealthy reasons: to boost a flagging self-esteem through being accepted and admired by those who are inferior, or to acquire a hollow sense of status or empty meaning, the end result will be that your self-esteem is reduced even further. Again, you have to begin by loving yourself; by respecting yourself enough to avoid those who will give you a false sense of worth, and by actively looking for people who will help you become a better, more fulfilled, and more loving person. This will set in motion an upward spiral. The higher your self-esteem, the more you will seek friends for healthy reasons; and the healthier your friendships, the higher will be your self-esteem.

Healthy reasons for having friends

Aristotle's definition of friendship accords with biblical descriptions, the classic one being that of David and Jonathan, whose love is described as surpassing the love of women. First, God wants friends to enjoy each other's company, to share pleasures and have fun together. This includes delighting in the other's achievements and successes, and so enhancing the other's sense of well-being. When we have low self-esteem, it is harder to rejoice with those who rejoice than it is to weep with those who weep.

Friendships are also intended to be reciprocal, not one-sided, with one person doing all the chasing or phoning, or with one taking the role of carer and the other of the cared-for — although there will be times in any friendship when this occurs. Friends must be generally useful to one another through the giving and receiving of love and the provision of mutual support. This includes sharing worries and concerns and giving each other practical help. It also involves stimulating each other's interests, helping each other see things from different perspectives and thereby expanding each other's soul.

True friendship also involves a common commitment to the good. God's intention is that friends should bring out the best in each other, helping each other develop their full potential and have an increasingly positive influence on society. This can be done through the giving and receiving of encouragement and direction, through gentle and constructive criticism and suggestions of better ways of doing things. Friends should also act as a check on each other. "Wounds from a friend can be trusted...." [3] A test of true friendship is whether or not you are a better person for having that friend.

Such friendships don't develop overnight. It takes time. And if you have moved around a lot it is particularly hard to keep starting all over again, especially as the older you get the more difficult it gets. Or maybe you have been badly hurt by a trusted friend and you don't want to risk getting hurt again. But healthy relationships involve being able to forgive, saying you're sorry, and being forgiven in return. If, for any reason, you have backed off from cultivating friends, or have never really had any true friends, you may have to set about making some acquaintances and, from there, developing a few close relationships.

How to make friends

If you want friends, you have to be friendly. Being friendly means being sincere, warm, open and direct, and genuinely interested in the other. You also have to appear friendly. You can do this by learning to smile, not shyly or tentatively, but confidently and spontaneously; by standing up straight and making eye contact; and by looking and sounding attentive and concerned. You can show interest by asking open-ended questions, those that require more than a yes or no answer — but don't pry. You don't have to be a talker. If you are genuinely attracted and engrossed by another, and want to learn from the other, you have a solid basis for developing a healthy friendship.

You may need to learn some communication skills, for example, how to express yourself clearly and avoid communication blocks, such as interrupting, monopolising or patronising. And you may need to practice being assertive, by using concise statements, rather than rambling ones; by using words that are cooperative rather than antagonistic; and by practicing making empathic sounds, ones that show that you can see from the other's point of view and understand the other's feelings. If you are having severe problems in this area, you may want to attend an assertiveness training course. Your local college or GP practice may be able to provide you with information about courses in your area.

However, learning social skills is not enough. If you want friends, you have to go out and find them; you have to be where people are. So, rather than sitting at home waiting for people to come to you, get involved in your church, join a club, attend evening classes.... And make the first move. For example, invite someone for coffee, suggest you go shopping together or attend some function. Don't let shyness be an excuse. Shyness is a symptom of low self-esteem, and as such has to be overcome.

You also have to be persistent. It takes two to form a friendship, and if others are also having problems with low self-esteem they may not immediately respond to your friendly overtures. Keep trying until you have built up a wide circle of different kinds of friends: friends of varying ages and with diverse interests who will accept you for what you are and stimulate you to grow and develop, emotionally and spiritually; friends who will enhance your sense of self-worth.

As you work at developing your social self, learning to receive and give love and form healthy relationships, you will find that your soul and spirit also develop. Remember, the biblical words for heart, soul and spirit are interchangeable. Also, love is at the root of everything because God *is* love. A healthy relationship not only makes us better people, but also brings us closer to God, enabling us to love as he loves.

> Love is patient, love is kind. It does not
> envy, it does not boast, it is not proud. It
> is not rude, it is not self-seeking, it is
> not easily angered, it keeps no record of
> wrongs. Love does not delight in evil
> but rejoices with the truth. It always
> protects, always trusts, always hopes,
> always perseveres. Love never fails. [4]

SUMMARY

A person's greatest need is love. But people with low self-esteem find it difficult to receive love, either from God or other people, and therefore cannot truly love themselves, God or others. There are different kinds of love, including "agapé", which is sacrificial and giving, and "phileo" which is to demonstrate a tender affection. Healthy love consists of knowledge, respect, responsibility and care. In order to boost a low self-esteem, we begin by learning how to receive love, especially from God. As we experience the warmth, security and freedom of God's love, we are enabled to love ourselves, and our love overflows to others.

It is love that enables us to become the type of people we want to be; we grow and develop only in the context of relationships. Nowadays, friends are especially important because technical advances and social changes have led to an increasing sense of alienation and isolation, with families often living many miles apart. However, when self-esteem is low it is difficult to make and keep friends, and there is a tendency to acquire the wrong type of friends, and for the wrong reasons. Friends should enjoy each other's company, be useful to one another, and share a common commitment to the good. In order to have such friends, we must first show ourselves friendly. When we are able to form healthy relationships, we become better people, and naturally feel better about ourselves, therefore, self-esteem is enhanced.

5

Self-esteem — the thinking self (mind)

I AM, THEREFORE I THINK

A mind to explore

The philosopher, Descartes, said, "Cogito ergo sum" — I think, therefore I am. The Bible teaches, I am, therefore I think. God created Adam first, and Adam's sense of curiosity and his ability to think and reason followed. However, during those times of extreme stress when nothing seems real, thinking itself is real, and proof of identity. So possibly both are true: we think because we are, and our ability to think makes us aware that we are, and who we are.

God made man an intelligent being, and through Christ there is a re-creation of a self which is being "...renewed in knowledge in the image of its Creator." [1] God intends us to explore, find out, and store up knowledge, and he blesses those who use their minds to find wisdom and understanding. This does not mean that we are all meant to be intellectuals; God has bestowed different gifts on different people. But everyone has the ability to use, and stretch, the mind.

There are basically two kinds of mental activity: rational, logical thinking, and creative, imaginative thinking, although, as with everything else, there is an overlap. Since the creative kind of thinking also involves the contemplations of the soul, this will be dealt with in Chapter 7. Here we will focus on rational, logical thought. In this area, the mind has three essential functions: reasoning, remembrance and resolve.

To reason is to think things through, play around with ideas, and come up with answers. We are told that Paul reasoned in the synagogue every Sabbath, and Peter exhorts us to have a reason for our faith. Our faith should not be a blind one, divorced from the thinking part of ourselves; on the contrary, the love we have for God should be with all our heart, soul, strength and mind. We love God because we have reason to love him.

To remember involves more than recalling to mind; it also involves assessing and applying. Jesus said, "Remember Lot's wife!" [2] which implies learning from her experience so that we don't hold onto those things that hinder our progress. In the case of the disciple Peter, when the cock crowed he remembered what Jesus had foretold: that he would deny him three times. And he wept bitterly. His mental recall touched also his heart and soul, and he resolved to make amends.

To resolve refers to attitude and will, the perfect example being Jesus. "Your attitude [mind] should be the same as that of Christ Jesus...." [3] He resolved to humble himself even unto death on the cross. Resolve, reasoning and remembering go together. For example, Joseph had it in mind to divorce the virgin Mary privately. His resolve came from a reasoned assessment of the situation, and from his remembering God's teaching on adultery, which, until the angel informed him otherwise, was the logical conclusion regarding Mary's pregnancy.

So, we are to use our ability to reason, remember and resolve in order to analyse and make sense of things. to assess people and situations and learn from them, to modify thoughts and ideas and create new ones, to explain, and to work out and decide on new courses of action and behaviour. We are also meant to use our mental abilities to explore God's Word and his works in creation.

His Word to explore

Paul commended the Bereans because they searched the Scriptures daily to check the veracity of his teaching. And we are told to present ourselves to God "...as one approved, a workman who does not need to be ashamed and who correctly handles the word of truth." [4] It is primarily through exploring God's Word that we discover what God is like factually, and get to know him experimentally; and it is through forming a relationship with God that we also discover our true inner selves.

His world to explore

God also wants us to use our minds to explore his works, because it is through creation, as well as through his Word, that we can discover and know God — and ultimately ourselves. God is clearly revealed in creation, to those who have eyes to see. "For since the creation of the world God's invisible qualities — his eternal power and divine nature — have been clearly seen, being understood from what has been made, so that men are without excuse." [5]

As people with low self-esteem tend to have a distorted perception of the world, and don't make use of their mental abilities, they don't see clearly or understand what is there in front of them. And this dulled and stunted thinking reduces low self-esteem even further. To some extent, we are all blind to the beauty of God and creation, and we all need to work at stimulating the natural curiosity and sense of wonder we had as children.

How strong is *your* sense of curiosity? Do you still have a child-like sense of wonder? Is your mind still active? It is very easy, especially in this TV age when learning is so often passive, to let our minds become lazy, to even allow ourselves to be spoon-fed from the pulpit instead of searching God's Word for ourselves. If this has happened to you, if you find it difficult to become interested in anything or have got into a mental rut, then it is also likely that you are drifting in life generally. And you cannot esteem yourself if you are not realising your potential. So prepare to take your mind in different directions by asking yourself, and finding out, how your curiosity came to be stifled in the first place, and your mind allowed to stagnate.

STUNTED CURIOSITY

Physical causes

Stunted curiosity goes hand in hand with low self-esteem, and like low self-esteem usually has its origins in childhood, although it can also arise in later life. Physical causes include those that affect perception, such as eye problems, and any form of visual-motor dysfunction. Thinking, of course, is also affected by brain damage or tumours, and by any prolonged, painful illness; it is hard to be interested in anything when pain is all-pervasive. But perhaps the most common physical cause of stunted curiosity is unrecognised and untreated dyslexia, especially if the sufferer has been made to think he is stupid. The feelings of frustration and inferiority, and the constant discouragements, can permanently stunt curiosity — unless help is sought.

Situational causes

The situational causes of stunted curiosity include adverse home conditions, either in childhood or in the present, such as cold, dirty surroundings, poverty, or overcrowding, with nowhere to study in peace and quiet. These conditions are especially harmful if there are also constant arguments. And if, during the school years, parents discouraged or even ridiculed learning, the effect may be a long-term stifling of curiosity.

Adverse school situations include overcrowded class-rooms, disruptive classmates, teachers who lack control or fail to make learning interesting, and teachers who, at the other extreme, are overpowering and intimidating. Lack of friends and bullying at school also contribute to inhibiting the desire to explore and find out.

Emotional causes

Curiosity can be stifled by parents who use their children to fulfil their own frustrated ambitions, or who are rigid and controlling. In order to retain their innate sense of curiosity, children have to be allowed to be themselves, and they need mental space: the freedom to ask questions and to think things through for themselves. Lack of such space is damaging to mental as well as emotional well-being. Equally damaging is lack of boundaries, or boundaries that are too broad. In order to explore, one has to feel safe.

Other causes of stunted curiosity include parents who have unrealistic expectations, who are overly critical, who place too much emphasis on grades, focus on mistakes, or provoke sibling rivalry. Especially damaging is telling a child he is stupid or that he will never amount to anything. In adulthood, constantly being made to feel stupid or inadequate by a domineering partner or other relative, or by a boss at work, and any prolonged mental disturbance, such as depression, can affect the desire to learn new things. One cannot be depressed and interested at the same time. The opposite also is true.

When people become convinced that they are stupid, that they are incapable of very much intelligent thought, they behave in ways that lead to yet more damaging effects. There is a downward spiral. In order to reverse this trend, begin by identifying those things that may have stifled your curiosity, then consider the long-term effects and ask yourself, is this me?

Effects of stunted curiosity

Stunted curiosity leads to a lack of learning, which in turn leads to feelings of being stupid or ignorant, and a sense of inadequacy; a feeling of being incapable of learning. There is also likely to be a fear of failure, and this can be so pervasive that there is a reluctance to try anything new, and a resistance even to the thought of having ambitions or setting goals. There may even be a general feeling of lethargy and depression. All of these reduce low self-esteem even further.

Stunted curiosity can also lead to the appearance of being stupid or ignorant, through a reluctance to join in conversations; a tendency to stand on the edge, fearful of saying anything that might sound silly or banal. The fear of coming out with something stupid, or making a mistake, may be so intense that the resulting nervousness actually leads to brainless, inane comments and clumsy, inappropriate actions. The end result, as there is an increasing withdrawal into the self, is likely to be fewer and less interesting friends, a boring marriage, and a dull, unsatisfying existence.

But stunted curiosity need not be permanent. The downward trend of shyness and withdrawal from people perceived to be interesting and intelligent can be reversed. It is possible, and necessary, whatever your age, to get back that insatiable curiosity that God intended you to have. People who have retained or regained their urge to explore and find out, and who seek to broaden their minds, are fulfilled and interesting people. And such people have high self-esteem.

If you seek to broaden your mind in a spirit of humility, then every piece of acquired knowledge will lead to God. But since God is known primarily through his Word, we will look first at how to explore — rather than simply reading — God's Word.

EXPLORING GOD'S WORD

What is God's Word?
The Bible is a library of sixty-six books. It was written over a period of 1,500 years in three different languages, and is inspired by God:

All Scripture is God-breathed [inspired] and
is useful for teaching, rebuking, correcting
and training in righteousness, so that the
man of God may be thoroughly equipped
for every good work. [6]

Approximately 60% of the Old Testament — and about the same
proportion of the Gospels and Acts — is historical narrative.
The Bible gives a linear, progressive view of history, with a
purpose and a goal: to reveal God's character and bring people
to salvation through faith in Christ, and to enable them to
develop and grow, so that they are able to live out their faith. In
addition, the Bible comprises genealogies, chronicles, laws,
poetry and proverbs, biographies, parables, sermons, theological
teaching (e.g. the Epistles) and prophecies. There is something for
everyone!

How to explore God's Word

You should read the individual books like any other
book: start at the start and read to the end. If you have been
depressed for a long time, or have simply got out of the habit of
using your mind, you may want to commence with the Gospels,
using a modern, easily understood translation, or by reading some
simple Bible study aids — or any good Christian literature that is
true to God's Word. With the help of a good concordance and
other teaching aids, such as a Bible dictionary, you can also use
the Bible as a reference book for studying a theme or topic, such
as love, or creation.

The Bible should always be understood in context; verses
should not be picked out at random, neither should you look for
the hidden meaning in a passage. Good interpretation seeks to
uncover the plain meaning. So ask yourself, how would this book
or passage have been understood at the time, and how does it fit
into the Bible as a whole? The golden rule of Bible interpretation
is, Scripture must be interpreted by Scripture.

When exploring God's Word, there are several things you
should consider. One of these is the literary context. Ask yourself,
is this passage to be taken literally or figuratively? Some parts of

73

the Bible, such as poetry, proverbs or parables, are not meant to be taken literally; other parts, such as historical narrative and doctrine, are. One of the effects of stunted curiosity is a tendency to focus on factual truth, to find it difficult, if not impossible, to think creatively and metaphorically. If this is your difficulty, perhaps you should commence with the Psalms, thinking about the metaphors used, the pictures they conjure up, and the metaphors you might use to describe the same situation or feeling. (This is the kind of thinking that also involves the soul.)

Consider also the historical context. Although the Bible can be read and grasped with no prior knowledge of Bible history, knowing something of the background will make the Scriptures more meaningful. Ask yourself, for example, when was the book or passage written and what was happening at the time, geographically, politically, socially and religiously? To whom was it written: to an entire nation, a group, an individual, to believers or unbelievers? And why was it written; what was the author's purpose? Was there a specific problem in the nation, the church, in an individual's life that needed to be dealt with? Was there a need for encouragement, or perhaps warning? These questions, and the search for answers, will not only give you a deeper understanding of truth, but exercise your mind, making you more mentally healthy and alert.

Exploring God's Word also means putting it into practice. Since the Bible is the Word of God, it should be read prayerfully, allowing the Holy Spirit to speak through its pages. And as he speaks, use your mind to consider the application, asking yourself how you can apply the original meaning to your own situation or that of your church or country. But don't be carried away by your imagination. Keep to the principle that what God intended his Word to mean to the original hearers is what he intends it to mean today. As you put God's Word into practice, you will discover its power, including its effect on self-esteem: "For the word of God is living and active." [7]

The effects of exploring God's Word

The Bible is a great promoter of healthy self-esteem because, through its pages, you will become increasing aware of

74

your standing in God, and of the greatness of his love for you. God's Word cleanses, heals, restores, gives instruction, makes you wise, enables you to grow — all things that improve the self. And, by stretching your mind, it enables you to make use of the mental abilities God has given you. Moreover, as you apply his Word to your life, you will build on a firm foundation and enhance your integrity as you become the person you want to be. It is with your feet planted firmly upon this foundation that you can safely explore God's world.

EXPLORING GOD'S WORLD

Reasons for exploring God's world

The Bible is full of exhortations to find out, test, and prove. We are even invited to put God to the test. God wants us to explore his world because it is through creation, as well as through Scripture, that God reveals himself. The Psalmist wrote:

> The heavens declare the glory of God;
> the skies proclaim the work of his hands.
> Day after day they pour forth speech;
> night after night they display knowledge.
> There is no speech or language where
> their voice is not heard. Their voice goes
> out into all the earth, their words to the
> ends of the world. [8]

Another reason for exploring God's world is to understand it so that we can effectively carry out God's command to care for and protect it. We can explore God's world through studying any of the sciences, defined as knowledge acquired through study and practice, such as ecology, geography, geology, or botany. The list is inexhaustible.

Also, God wants us to ponder (think about) his works because he has made the world for us to enjoy. "Great are the works of the LORD; they are pondered by all who delight in them." [9] When we muse on God's works, we cannot help but sing

75

for joy. In other words, using our minds to explore God's works should be fun. Whatever your interests in life, God also wants you to enjoy them for their own sakes.

If you find it difficult to enjoy things for their intrinsic value, or if you often find yourself thinking or saying, "I'm bored — I've nothing to do," you need to question yourself. It is interesting that in some languages, such as German, the verb "to bore" is reflexive: "I am boring myself." So, stop boring yourself and, while respecting the boundaries God has set, for example, around the world of the occult, start using your mind. There is a world out there waiting to be discovered.

Some examples of those who explored God's world

Throughout history, the most amazing discoveries have often been made by people who used their minds in obedience to God's command. The classic examples are the four leaders of the Scientific Revolution: Copernicus, Kepler, Galileo and Newton. They all had a strong faith in God and explored the universe for his glory and the benefit of mankind.

Copernicus firmly believed that the universe was made by a supremely good and orderly Creator. He revolutionised science with his declaration that the sun, not the earth, was the centre of the universe. Kepler's belief in the harmony of creation, which he termed "a sacred sermon", led to his laying the foundation for modern theoretical astronomy. Galileo believed that God has given us two books, one of nature the other of Scripture, and he became renowned for the construction and use of telescopes. And Newton, who believed that no sciences are better attested than the religion of the Bible, was the one who discovered gravity.

Later, the early Protestants actively encouraged, not only the study of the Bible, but also the study of God's works in nature, with the result that many of the leading scientists in history have been committed Christians. These include all the early members of the Royal Society, founded in England in 1661. The three most influential founder members of the oldest natural history society in the world, in London, were Quakers. Most famous of the Quaker scientists was John Dalton (1766-1844), founder of the chemical atomic theory.

Unlike the above, your pursuit of knowledge in order to glorify God and benefit mankind will probably not result in anything earth shattering. But don't let this make you discount your own explorations, or your achievements. Whatever you do, however small, to enhance your own self will also have a positive effect on those around you.

The effects of exploring God's world
The more we use and exercise our brains, whether through studying God's Word or his works — which means any subject under the sun — the more they are able to accomplish. We are therefore protected from stagnation and senility, and possibly from depression.

The more we know, the more we want to know: our curiosity is stimulated and our minds broadened. Therefore, we are launched on an upward spiral that will result in an increased appreciation of all that God has given us, including our own mental abilities. But, we must be careful not to become conceited in our minds. True learning results in a deeper realisation that our short time on this earth is insufficient to discover all that God has done and is doing. And it results in a greater awareness of how very little we know, with a corresponding humility.

Therefore, use every opportunity to use and develop your mind. And rediscover the curiosity you had as a child so that, like a child, you can stand in wonder and amazement before our wonderful Creator.

Expanding your personal horizons

You can stimulate your curiosity by first recognising and accepting that God created your mind, and that he made you responsible for its development. Then, using all five senses, take every opportunity to look, listen, touch, taste and smell. Go to the library or website, start reading, checking things out in dictionaries, encyclopedias, and the like. Begin where your interests are and branch out from there, and use materials at the right level: too easy and you'll get bored, too difficult and you'll get discouraged. Learning should be fun.

You may be telling yourself that you don't have time; that you have a family to care for, a demanding job, or both. We all have periods in our lives when we feel overburdened by responsibilities, and we get frustrated at the lack of time for ourselves. But maybe you should question if, in fact, you have allowed your responsibilities to take over in order to avoid having to confront your fear of trying anything new, or of being what you really want to be.

If you don't know what your interests are, or what you really want to be, ask yourself, if you had the choice of any career in the world (and there were no hindrances, such as age, lack of training or qualifications, home responsibilities), what would you do? It might help to write a diary of your life: the kinds of work you have done, your hobbies and accomplishments, noting what you do in your spare time, what you enjoy doing, and what you are good at. And think about your dreams and fantasies, asking yourself what you would like to achieve before you die.

78

You may be contemplating broadening your interests just so you can assist your children with their schoolwork, or to become a more compelling and self-assured person. But as your curiosity increases, and you become more aware of the vastness and wonder of God's creation, you might find yourself dissatisfied with what you have accomplished in life and wanting to embark on new courses of study, try new experiences, travel, meet new people.... Once you come to grasp the wonder of the human mind, and commit your mind to God for his use, there is no knowing where God will lead.

Whatever reason you have for stretching your mind, you must have goals — both short-term, easily reachable goals and long-term goals. Having goals means that you have hope for the future, something to look forward to, a purpose in life that will keep you going through the bad times, when self-esteem is at its nadir. Having goals implies that you have some belief in your ability to reach those goals, therefore, self-esteem is given a boost. And having goals protects from mental illness, especially depression.

So, if you have been robbed of the natural curiosity you had as a child, work at restoring it by stirring up your mind and using it to explore God's Word and his works in creation. Then, as the thinking part of you becomes more active and your interests increase, you will have a reason to keep your body healthy, your heart and soul will be enlarged and, if you are using your mind for God's glory and the benefit of others, your spirit too will be enriched.

SUMMARY

God has given all of us innate curiosity and minds that are able to reason, remember and resolve. And he wants us to use our minds to wisely and thoughtfully explore his Word and his works in creation. However, curiosity may have become stifled through physical disability, adverse home or school conditions, or emotional damage occurring during the childhood years, or in adulthood. The result is lowered self-esteem because of the feeling, and appearance, of ignorance and stupidity. But curiosity can be regained and learning ability enhanced. The first step is to accept that God has given us brains and to commit our minds to him for his use. Then, inspired by the examples of godly scientists in the past, every effort should be made to explore, find out, and contemplate all that God has done and made, to glorify God and benefit others, including ourselves.

6

Self-esteem — the physical self (body)

OUR BODIES: GOOD OR EVIL

Some misconceptions

People with low self-esteem tend to have more problems with their body image than with any other aspect of themselves. There are two main problem areas, one of which is the tendency to see our bodies as evil. This has arisen through the influence of philosophy.

The idea that the body, and the entire material world, is evil — and that the body is the prison house of the soul — entered Christian thought through Platonism and Gnosticism, a heretical movement which arose in the first century. Gnostics ("gnosis" means "to know") thought of evil in terms of disturbance or dysfunction rather than moral wrong, and believed that this badness was located in the body, therefore the way to overcome it was to transcend the body. Gnostics further taught that the way to know God is first to know oneself, which, as has been discussed, is potentially dangerous; we know ourselves primarily through knowing God. Gnosticism is a direct forerunner of Buddhism, and elements of it are found in some modern psychology theories.

If, consciously or unconsciously, you think of your body as essentially bad, this misconception is most likely to have come to you via your parents, or significant others, mainly because of how they viewed sexuality. If sex was a taboo subject, something not very nice that wasn't talked about, or if you were sexually abused — which includes being inappropriately exposed to sexual activity — you will have found it easier to embrace this ancient Gnostic view of the body as it is found, albeit in disguised form, in some parts of the Christian Church today. Discovering what the Bible says about the body is the first step towards correcting this misconception.

Some biblical truths

The word "soma" in the New Testament, usually translated "body", has three basic meanings. First, it can mean the physical part of man, that is the substance of the body. Or it may refer to the complete man: body, soul and spirit. Or, it can refer to the weaker or sinful element of human nature. In this instance, it is interchangeable with the word "sarx" or "flesh". For example, "I know that nothing good lives in me, that is, in my sinful nature [K.J. 'flesh']." [1] But whatever the meaning, the body itself is not considered evil, or even as the source of evil. On the contrary, Jesus said,

> "For from within, out of men's hearts, come evil thoughts, sexual immorality, theft, murder, adultery, greed, malice, deceit, lewdness, envy, slander, arrogance and folly. All these evils come from inside and make man 'unclean'." [2]

Paul similarly exhorted the Ephesians not to live as the Gentiles do "...in the futility of their thinking [mind]." [3] Sin does not come from the body, but from the heart and mind.

Misconceptions about our bodies and self-esteem

If we think of our bodies as sinful, we will either ill-treat them or ignore them. And the more we degrade them, the more we will think them evil. This downward spiral will be particularly manifested in the areas of sensuality — such as guilt about pleasant physical sensations, like enjoying a leisurely bath or lying in the garden — and sexuality. Many sexual difficulties in marriage arise because of the mistaken belief, that may be lurking in a corner of the mind, that it is wrong to enjoy each other's bodies.

On the other hand, if we accept that God sees our bodies

82

as essentially good, we will respect and care for them, and allow ourselves to enjoy them. (Enjoyment is not the same as indulgence.) And the more we look after our bodies, the more we will perceive them as good, sending self-esteem spiralling upwards.

Have you thought of your body as sinful, or regarded it merely as an unimportant outer case to house the all-important soul? If so, these misconceptions need to be cleared away before you can even begin to improve your body image. But perhaps also you have a misconception about your body's appearance.

OUR BODIES: BEAUTIFUL OR UGLY

How we see ourselves

The second main problem area with regard to our bodies is the tendency to see them as ugly. And this comes from the influence of society. Christians are not immune from the feeling of comparing badly with others, especially those in the media. But Christians, unlike the general population, tend to spiritualise the problem, telling themselves that it doesn't matter what they look like because, "Man looks at the outward appearance, but the LORD looks at the heart." [4] However, the outward appearance is important for the very reason that this is what man looks at. Certainly, God does place prior importance on our inner beauty, but he does not disregard the body.

Our perceptions of our bodies are based initially on how our parents, or other family members, viewed us. For instance, if we were constantly told that we were ugly, looked a mess, were too skinny, too fat, these perceptions are likely to persist; unless we are fortunate enough to find a partner who makes us feel good about our bodies, enabling us to challenge these parental views. To a lesser extent, we are also affected by how our teachers and childhood friends viewed us.

In addition to childhood influences, we continue to be greatly affected by how society at large evaluates us. Constant bombardment from TV, magazines, and other media can make us feel that we don't measure up. But societal fashions change, and it helps to remind ourselves of this. For example, Rubens' idea of beauty was of women who were decidedly rounded; a contrast to the 1940s' and 1950s' Hollywood ideal or the later Twiggy look. While not everyone is beautiful according to current evaluations, everyone has something beautiful about them, in part, because what we are on the inside shows on the outside.

And what about you? How do you see yourself? Maybe there is a part of you that you don't like, such as uneven teeth or fat thighs, and every time you look in the mirror all you see is teeth or thighs. It could be helpful for you here to try the mirror exercise, which you may need to keep repeating until you are able to see yourself objectively.

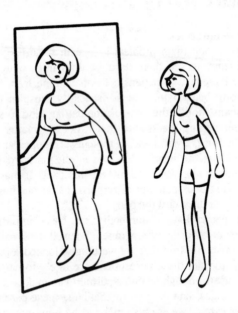

When you are alone, and unlikely to be disturbed, stand naked in front of a full-length mirror and notice your overall reaction. Then, starting with your hair, assess each specific part of your body, noting your likes and dislikes and listing these in two columns; for example, your eyes, nose, hands.... The likes should be accepted and appreciated, while the dislikes can be reassessed and listed in two further columns: the disliked parts that can be changed, and the disliked parts you're stuck with but that can be minimised or detracted from. While you work at changing how you see yourself, appreciating your good points and altering those not-so-good ones, also take a look at how God sees you.

How God sees us

God saw that what he had created was very good. And he has not changed his mind. True, our bodies have been affected by the Fall, our original beauty has suffered distortions and deformities, and we are all prey to the ravages of time. But we are God's workmanship, and in his eyes we are beautiful. David wrote,

> For you created my inmost being; you knit me together in my mother's womb. I praise you because I am fearfully and wonderfully made; your works are wonderful, I know that full well. [5]

The material world, including our bodies, is pleasing to God, and we should endeavour to keep it so.

Body perception and self-esteem

As with the perception of our bodies as evil, seeing them as ugly will have a negative effect on the way we treat them. If we think of ourselves as unattractive, we will, consciously or unconsciously, alter our behaviour accordingly: we will avoid people or eye contact, cringe, cower, shrink into a corner.... So we will appear small and shrivelled, becoming nonentities. We are likely also to dress dowdily in order to hide our bodies, or to make no effort with appearance because of the faulty opinion that it's not worth it. This will create a dull, boring impression, with a corresponding feeling of self-consciousness, that is, the feeling of being observed but not approved. This, like the conception of our bodies as evil, will set into motion a downward spiral.

85

You can reverse this trend by altering your thinking about your body, and by making some small changes to the way you come across to others, by standing up straight, holding your head up, smiling and looking people in the eye. As you do this, even without any major reorganisation of your wardrobe, you will start to feel and look more attractive, and your self-esteem will be enhanced. But you are far more likely to succeed if you also grasp the truth that we have a special responsibility for our bodies.

RESPONSIBILITY FOR OUR BODIES

Reasons for being responsible

We are responsible for all of creation, and this includes keeping and preserving our own bodies. In order to do this, we have to know them, that is become aware of them, listening to what they are telling us: to rest, have a break, to calm down, get some exercise.... In order to be responsible, we also have to respect and appreciate our bodies, and look after them. These four requirements — knowledge, respect, responsibility and care — add up to the fact that we have to love our bodies. Love is manifested in two ways: preserving, as far as possible, the efficient functioning of our bodies, and maintaining the pleasing appearance of our bodies.

We are responsible for the efficient functioning of our bodies so that we can carry out, to the best of our ability, God's command to do good works, and to care for all creation. Also, God wants us to be vibrant and glowing with health. He wants us to experience his power so that our youth is renewed like the eagle's, so that we metaphorically leap like a deer on the mountains. Being human, of course we become tired and weary, we get sick, and we grow old. This is a result of the Fall; it is not necessarily because of personal sin. But if weakness and lethargy, sickness and premature ageing arise because of our own neglect, then we are accountable.

We are responsible for keeping ourselves looking attractive because God loves beauty, and it hurts him to see us looking miserable and downtrodden. He himself is beautiful — although not in a physical sense — and his beauty is manifested in creation. God wants us, as much as possible, to radiate his goodness and loveliness; and we can do this only as we develop our inner beauty and ensure that our bodies reflect it unhindered. Beauty and health go together. We cannot look good if we constantly feel tired and ill. So perhaps our primary responsibility is to keep our bodies in good working order.

Responsibility for the efficient functioning of our bodies

Since God wants us to be healthy, we should work at keeping fit. But we must keep the balance correct: the most care must be devoted to spiritual well-being. Paul wrote, "For physical training is of some value, but godliness has value for all things, holding promise for both the present life and the life to come." [6]

Paul was probably referring to the new Greek gymnasiums which were then all the rage in Palestine, and to which young men like the half-Greek Timothy were drawn. What we consider physical training — aerobics, keep-fit, etc. — was not necessary for a people who were engaged in manual labour, who didn't travel everywhere by car, and who didn't spend their evenings slumped in front of the TV. If "couch potatoes" had existed in Paul's time, he would probably have said that physical exercise is of great value!

In order to preserve the efficient functioning of our bodies, it is essential also that we have periods of rest and relaxation. In times of turmoil and stress, God wants to lead us by still waters, so that our soul — and body — can be restored. Jesus often exhorted his disciples to come away with him to a quiet place and get some rest.

Besides physical exercise and rest, we need to ensure that we have a healthy, well-balanced diet, avoiding gluttony but enjoying all that God has provided. Paul warned that in the last days there would be deceiving spirits who would order people to "...abstain from certain foods, which God created to be received with thanksgiving...." [7] He went on to say that everything God created is good, and nothing is to be rejected if it is received with thanksgiving. God has given us a wonderful diversity of food, not only to build up our bodies and keep them healthy, but also for our enjoyment. The Psalmist was one who could rejoice in God's provision. He wrote, "He makes grass grow for the cattle, and plants for man to cultivate — bringing forth food from the earth: wine that gladdens the heart of man, oil to make his face shine, and bread that sustains his heart." [8]

So, in order to keep our bodies functioning, we are responsible for getting the right amount of exercise, for ensuring that we have times of rest and relaxation, and for having healthy, well-balanced diets. However, people with low self-esteem tend to fall down on all three of these: they tend not to exercise; they tend to feel guilty if they are not rushing around, constantly doing; and they tend to overeat, eat the wrong things, or starve themselves.

How well do you score on these three areas? Do you exercise sufficiently? And are you able, like Mary the sister of Martha, to stop bustling around and stop, to simply be still and listen? Are you overweight or do you have a tendency to starve yourself? As you work at improving these three areas, your self-esteem will naturally be enhanced. And this in turn will increase your desire to keep your body in shape — and to keep it looking good.

Responsibility for the pleasing appearance of our bodies

God wants us to keep ourselves, not only as fit as possible, but also as attractive as possible. But again, we must keep the balance correct: true beauty comes from within, and we must seek first and foremost to develop our inner glory. However, we must not forget that man looks on the outward appearance, and all that this implies. While not being conformed to the world's views on beauty, we must not neglect the adorning of our outer selves.

The Greek word for adorn, "kosmeo", is the verbal form of the noun "kosmos", the universe which God created, loves and continues to uphold. Also, it is the word from which we get the English "cosmetic". "Kosmeo" literally means to arrange, put in order. Archeology has shown that, because of the dry climate, Jewish men and women cared for their skin with oils and perfumes. In addition, Jewish ladies used red dyes for lips, cheeks, finger and toenails. And both sexes adorned themselves with jewellery.

Such adornments are described in the wedding song (Psalm 45). Jewish brides adorned themselves for their husbands with gold, silver, precious stones, fragrant perfumes and beautifully embroidered clothes. God is described as similarly adorning the unfaithful Jerusalem. His condemnation was not of her beauty, but of her trusting in her beauty and using it for evil purposes. Like Jewish brides, the bride of Christ is told to adorn herself for her heavenly bridegroom with fine clothes, jewellery and perfumes.

Taking responsibility for the pleasing appearance of our bodies means, above all, keeping it clean and fresh. John Wesley maintained that cleanliness is next to godliness. This includes keeping our bodies smelling nice. "Perfume and incense bring joy to the heart..." [9] It also includes arranging, putting in order, or caring for our hair, which is a woman's glory. And, it means keeping our bodies warm and well groomed through the care of our clothes, which God has promised to provide. It is written of the wife of noble character that, "When it snows, she has no fear for her household; for all of them are clothed in scarlet. She makes coverings for her bed; she is clothed in fine linen and purple." [10] God's first creation, light, was in effect the creation of colour and beauty.

Perhaps you have nursed a misconception about outward beauty, along with the belief that it is selfish to meet your own needs. Changing this misconception is a prerequisite for changing the way you look. Next, take a look at your general grooming, your hair, your clothes, and the way you adorn yourself. (Adornment should enhance, not deceive.) Then, start putting yourself in order, so that you can offer back to God a body that is pleasing to him.

Responsibility for the offering of our bodies

Our bodies are not our own. The apostle Paul wrote, "Do you not know that your body is a temple of the Holy Spirit, who is in you, whom you have received from God? You are not your own; you were bought at a price. Therefore honour God with your body." [11]

We do not own our bodies any more than we own the rest of creation; rather, we are stewards of our bodies. And as we take responsibility for them, knowing, respecting and caring for them, we should, at the same time, offer them back to God: "Therefore, I urge you, brothers, in view of God's mercy, to offer your bodies as living sacrifices, holy and pleasing to God — this is your spiritual act of worship." [12]

In order to present our bodies to God, we must accept that they are not our own, and recognise the responsibility and privilege of our stewardship. And, we must be able to thank God for our bodies: we cannot present something that we do not appreciate and value. It is only as we acknowledge that our bodies are essentially good and beautiful, and work at keeping them so, that the offering of our bodies will be truly pleasing to God.

If you have neglected your body, its efficient functioning or pleasing appearance, then you will need, first of all, to resolve to work at improving your body in either, or both, of these areas. There is no set standard that you have to reach before you can present it back to God. As with any growth and development, enhancing your body is a life-long task. This, and giving your body to God, should be a simultaneous, on-going process, an offering of love. Love is always pleasing to God.

IMPROVING OUR BODIES

Exercise and rest

If you look good you will feel good. And to look good you have to keep your body in shape. One way is through physical exercise. If you haven't exercised for a long time, or are seriously out of condition, then consult your doctor before you begin. Physical exercise improves the stamina of the heart and lungs and protects against coronary disease. It also improves the circulation, keeps back, neck and joints supple, and tightens and strengthens muscles. In other words, exercise improves stamina, suppleness and strength. It also helps you stay slim, makes you feel good physically and mentally, and enables you to combat stress.

The best all-round activities — those that improve cardio-respiratory fitness, increase the range of movements, strengthen muscle and reduce fat — are aerobics, gymnastics, and swimming. Others include walking, jogging, dancing, cycling, court sports, and calisthenics. Vigorous exercise should always be preceded by a few minutes gentle bending and stretching.

Besides physical exercise, we need to ensure that we have times of relaxation and rest. So take time to do the things you enjoy, such as walking, sitting on the beach, or simply lying in the garden. If you have a very busy lifestyle, then allowing yourself ten minutes here and there to do absolutely nothing can prevent overload. Or try this quickie relaxation technique, which can be carried out at your desk or between household tasks: take three deep breaths, exhaling slowly. Then, slowly stretch, close your eyes and let your whole body go completely limp. Stay limp for a minute or two. Then, take three more deep breaths before commencing work again. As you learn to take care of your body, and allow it times to unwind, you will feel better, and esteem yourself more.

Diet

To be healthy, both physically and mentally, we need the right balance of calories, dietary fibre, water and nutrients; this last includes proteins, carbohydrates, fats, vitamins and minerals. These are the raw materials needed to build and repair the body.

If you need to lose weight, don't go on a crash diet. Lose weight slowly and sensibly. If you are seriously overweight get your doctor's advice first. Otherwise, follow these general dietary tips: replace saturated-fat red meat and dairy products with nutrient-rich beans, other vegetables, and fruit. Replace dairy fat with polyunsaturated vegetable oil. Reduce salt and sugar, eat more fibre, and drink more water. Finally, learn to eat more slowly and enjoy your food. And learn when to stop. Using God's provision of food wisely will ensure that you have a body that you are happy with.

Appearance

People who feel plain or ugly tend to think that it's not worth making an effort with appearance, or wearing nice things. But, people who look plain or ugly usually do so because of the way they dress. First impressions count, and what is seen initially is the overall person, especially the face, hair, and clothes. If you are wearing dark or dowdy clothes, you will give the impression of being dowdy and a nonentity. So brighten yourself up. If you don't know what colours suit you, then get together with a friend and try on each other's clothes. You might surprise yourself.

You needn't go to a lot of expense. Just making a few minor changes can do wonders for self-esteem: a new dress, a different haircut, a change of make-up. But remember, cosmetics are meant to enhance what God has given us, not to disguise our natural features. There are some women who don't need make-up; others feel uncomfortable wearing it. With this, as with everything else, it is essential to know your own beliefs and values, and to adhere to them. But it is also important to be flexible enough to question your motives. If you don't wear make-up because you don't think you're worth it, then you have a self- esteem problem and need to re-think your views.

One view that should be challenged is the one that, since

God accepts us just as we are, it doesn't matter how we look. This is a misunderstanding of what acceptance means. A loving human parent accepts his or her children just as they are: looking like nothing on earth when they've just got out of bed, in tatty old jeans or grubby gardening clothes. But they would be hurt if their children made an effort to look nice for others but consistently took no trouble for them, because, "It's only Mum and Dad." God wants us to make the best of ourselves so that he can enjoy looking at us.

So, in order to improve the way you perceive your body, accept it as essentially good and beautiful, and work at keeping it as fit and attractive as possible. If you need to step up the exercise or go on a diet, look on these as ways of serving and pleasing God. He is not only concerned about your soul and spirit, he is also concerned about your physical self.

SUMMARY

Two misconceptions about our bodies have entered Christian thought. One is the belief that our bodies are evil; the influence of philosophy. The other is the belief that our bodies are ugly; the influence of society. We need to challenge these misconceptions — which probably came to us via our parents — by first discovering how God views our bodies. God created them, and he created them good and beautiful. And because God made them, they belong to him; we are merely stewards, responsible for their efficient functioning and pleasing appearance, and for offering them back to God, holy and pure.

We can keep our bodies healthy through taking sufficient exercise, having periods of rest and relaxation, and eating a healthy, well-balanced diet. We can keep them looking good through paying attention to cleanliness and general grooming, and through humbly and gratefully adorning them in ways that will best reflect our inner beauty. The more we respect and care for our bodies, becoming increasingly aware of their reactions to the daily stresses of life, and responding to their functional and aesthetic needs, the better we will feel about them, and the greater will be our self-esteem.

7

Self-esteem — the sensing self (soul)

WHAT IS THE SOUL?

The life principle

The soul, as discussed in Chapter 2, can be defined according to the Hebrew "nepes" as "possessing life", or the "life principle". In this respect it is the essential self, and as such is intangible and indefinable. The ancient Celtic belief that it was important for every individual to discover his soul's unique shape is akin to the modern concept of self-actualisation. It is only possible to truly esteem ourselves if we are truly being ourselves — living our lives in obedience to our own inner voice — rather than trying to copy someone else.

The seat of emotions

The soul is also described, by both the Hebrew "nepes" and the Greek "psyche", as being the source of emotions. It is that part of a human concerned with experiencing, sensing, feeling and desiring. These words for soul can also refer to man's higher nature, or conscience, which is manifested in moral behaviour. When they are used in this sense they are interchangeable with the Bible words translated as "spirit". Although emotions and behaviours may be recognised and labelled, their source, being one and the same with the primal urge towards life and fulfilment, is more obscure.

The source of creativity

It is at the source that one touches also on the spiritual: the divinity within, which is essentially creative. In this respect the soul is concerned with creative thinking. There are different kinds, or levels, of thinking. Rational thought and will are generally associated with the mind; the creative thinking of the soul could be described as intuition or perception. Creative thinking occurs most often in dream states: during actual dreams or when we daydream.

Since, at the deepest levels, the psychological and spiritual merge, any devaluing or demeaning of the soul affects also our spiritual well-being. Therefore, the development of the soul is of special importance for acquiring a healthy self-esteem. As the soul is concerned with life, emotions and creativity, attention must be paid to all three in order to develop the soul. But, when self-esteem is low, life can seem a burden and we lose the wonder of simply being, while emotions can seem so overpowering that there is a desire to repress them or blot them out. And creativity is stifled.

And what about your soul? Are you celebrating life, living it to the full? Are you in touch with your feelings: able to recognise and name them, and allow yourself to experience them? It is impossible to control emotions, and express them appropriately, without first being aware of them. And are you able to tap into your source of creativity, to realise your full creative potential? If you have difficulty in these areas, then start listening to yourself. Identify your feelings, and shades of feelings, and take notice of what your dreams and daydreams are telling you. As you do so, your inner voice will probably help you identify the basic problem, which is one of smallness.

PROBLEMS OF THE SOUL

We have a shrunken God

In this high-tech age with its throw-away mentality, there is less awareness of eternal values; of the need to simply be quiet, to meditate, to reflect on God and his greatness, and open up to his immeasurable love and power. The result is that God has become limited and confined. We see him as the God of the Bible, or the God of the Christian Church. But God is so much bigger. At the dedication of his temple, Solomon prayed, "The heavens, even the highest heavens, cannot contain you." [1] And

God declared to the prophet, Jeremiah, "Do not I fill heaven and earth?" [2] If we have eyes to see, we can recognise and experience God everywhere we look.

We live in a shrunken world

Modern technology and travel have resulted in a "global village". Our world has shrunk. But in spite of this, people today tend to be isolated. Christians especially seem to have lost the sense of community: with saints past and present, and with the entire created world. This is demonstrated in our choruses. The traditional hymns that used to magnify God through creation, and contemplate man's place and function in the created world, have given place to choruses that emphasise *me*: what God is doing for *me*, what *I* feel.

This self-centredness is due in part to the influence of the 20th century focus on the individual, and on some modern psychology theories that rightly aim for self-actualisation, but without regard to man's place in the greater scheme of things. It is only as man loses himself in God's greater purposes that he will find (actualise) himself. We have to lose our soul in order to find it.

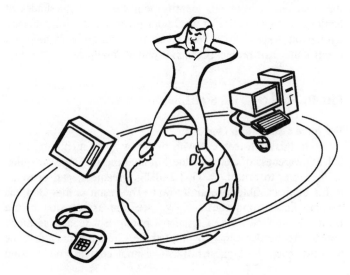

Man has shrunk himself

It is not only God and his works that have been belittled, but man himself. The nineteenth century was the age of the machine, when man started becoming superfluous, or at best, a cog in a machine. And with increasing mass production, craftsmanship became devalued and ancient skills were lost. The late twentieth century was the age of the computer; and now, with the emphasis on academic knowledge and information exchange, we are forgetting how to simply be. Our souls, the source of life, are dying as they are pushed to one side, cramped into tiny pockets of space, which are all that are left in this materialistic world. We are also forgetting how to feel. We talk a lot about feelings, but we have a limited repertoire of words to describe them: words such as love, hate; happiness, sadness; calm, anger; confidence and fear. It is small wonder that we sometimes find it difficult to control our feelings when we have turned ourselves into robots.

In order to be fully human, the soul needs space and a deep awareness of the full range of human emotions. But when self-esteem is low, the associated insecurity leads to a tendency to compartmentalise: to put everything — God, the world and our own feelings — into tidy little boxes with neat little labels. If, on reflection, you realise that you have organised your world into little boxes, then as you read the next section, open your mind and soul to the greatness of God and his works. Learn to experience, sense, creatively think about, and emotionally respond to every aspect of his creation. And work at rejecting the old voices of the past: the voices that belittled you and put you down. Instead, start believing in the greatness of your potential. You are capable of far more than you can ever imagine.

ENLARGING THE SOUL

The greatness of God

In order to enlarge the soul, we must first discover the greatness of God. Although we find God primarily through the Bible, he is so much bigger than this; he reaches from eternity to eternity; he fills heaven and earth. Jesus lived and died in time, but he was the lamb slain from the creation of the world. And his death was foreshadowed in the Old Testament; the entire sacrificial system was a wonderful picture of sin and death, redemption and resurrection. But this picture is not confined to the Bible. We can see it in creation, and in the myths of all cultures. The picture was there from the beginning. In order to grasp something of the greatness of God, we will move back in time to prehistory, to the world of mythology.

Myths, which belong essentially to the realms of the soul, have become distorted as a result of the Fall. But if we can see beyond the distortions to the original, we will see God, because God has revealed himself through myth. For example, myths tell the story of creation, of a primal pair who disobeyed God, of the sacrificial death of God's son, and of resurrection. Paul wrote regarding those who have never heard of Jesus, that they are without excuse because God has also clearly revealed himself through creation, and through an innate knowledge of the truth:

> ...what may be known about God is plain to
> them [pagans], because God has made it plain
> to them. For since the creation of the world
> God's invisible qualities — his eternal power
> and divine nature — have been clearly seen,
> being understood from what has been made,
> so that men are without excuse. [3]

The Greek phrase translated, "has made it plain to them", means "manifest among them" or "in them"; that is, "in their minds". The psychoanalyst, Carl Jung, proposed the theory that man has a collective consciousness; he believed that deep in our psyche (soul) we have an awareness of an unknown prehistoric past. C.S. Lewis suggested that what we actually share is an innate, intuitive knowledge of sin and God's plan of redemption; a knowledge that is manifested through dreams and myths. This theory is not without foundation. Missionaries have often reported that tribes hitherto unreached by the Gospel have already known, albeit in a confused form, the story of Jesus.

Myths throughout the world, of every tribe and tongue and

nation, tell the story of Jesus. But we will look at just a few, from a group of ancient eastern Mediterranean countries. These tell the stories of the corn (fertility) gods, Osiris of Egypt, Attis of Phrygia, Adonis of Syria, and Dionysus of Greece. According to the myths, these gods were all associated with crops, especially corn, and with the vine, and their symbols were bread and wine. They were all associated with a sacrificial animal. Attis, and possibly Dionysus, was born of a virgin. All of them died violent deaths at the time of the spring equinox, i.e. Easter, and rose again from the dead. And from the blood of these gods, new life sprang forth.

Some scholars think that these stories merely demonstrate death and resurrection in nature, and have gone so far as to suggest that Jesus' death and resurrection was merely a symbolic portrayal of this natural cycle. But if God created nature, and if Jesus was slain from the foundation of the earth, then surely it is the other way round: the theme of death and resurrection in nature — and the myths connected with it — demonstrates the death and resurrection of Christ!

When we are able to understand, if only dimly, that the mark of God's design is everywhere, then our souls cannot help but open up to the wonder and greatness of it. And the more we wonder at God's kindness and goodness to man, at the enormous privilege of having his truth imprinted on our souls, the more humbly we will thank him for making us what we are.

If you have limited God, seeing him only as the God of the Bible, or worse, as the God of part of the Bible — for example, the righteous, avenging God of the Old Testament; or the kind, loving God of the New — then take time to ponder the amazing truth that God is everywhere, that he inhabits eternity, and that the story of redemption is written on the heart of man and has been told in countless ways from the very dawn of time.

The greatness of God's world
The soul can also be developed through increased knowledge of creation and man's place in it, as well as through increased awareness of God, and by carrying out our God-given responsibilities towards the entire created world. If we are not

taking our responsibilities seriously, then we cannot truly esteem ourselves; we fall short of what we know in our innermost beings is our function in life, and a great honour. Neither can we truly esteem ourselves if we are abusing or neglecting God's creation. God has commanded us to subdue and rule the earth: to exercise mastery. Being a master means to serve, as Christ demonstrated. We are responsible for conservation, maintenance, avoidance of pollution, harmony, and the wise use of resources.

In order to carry out our responsibilities efficiently, we need first to be aware of creation and get to know it, recognising that the world is God's house. The Greek word for house is "oikos", from which we get the words "ecology" and "economy". The study of ecology is the study of God's house. We need, then, to develop an awareness of every aspect of God's house, whether mountains and valleys, beaches and seas, plants and trees, or living creatures — as did Adam.

God brought all the beasts of the field and the birds of the air to Adam, to see what he would call them. This was not merely labelling; rather, God was placing trust in Adam's ability to be aware of and recognise the shape of every creature's inner soul, and name it accordingly. As a result of the Fall, and especially in this day and age, we seem to have lost the ability to recognise and appreciate others' unique strengths and abilities, whether human or animal. So it is not surprising that we also have difficulty recognising and appreciating ourselves.

In order to develop awareness, we have to learn to stand still, to stop rushing around and give our mind and soul breathing space. As we stand still, awareness will be heightened through increased use of all the senses God has given us: sight, hearing, touch, taste, and smell, as well as the inner senses, which include insight and intuition. As we then take notice of our perceptions and their emotional effect on us, we will also become more aware of a greater variety of feelings within ourselves. And the more we recognise and respond to our feelings, the greater will be our sensitivity to others, and the more we will be able to respond to God in worship and praise.

In addition to becoming aware of creation, God also wants us to respect the strengths and abilities of all his creatures. In

Proverbs, for example, we are told to consider the ant. And God responded to Job's complaints by broadening his understanding and appreciation of creation, asking him to consider the miracle of the sea and clouds, the marvel of the earth and the stars of the heaven; the wonder of the rain, hail and snow; and the incredible diversity of animals, from the donkey to the hippopotamus. As a result, Job was able to admit, "Surely I spoke of things I did not understand, things too wonderful for me to know." [4]

Appreciation and respect include enjoying. The Psalmist wrote, "For you make me glad by your deeds, O LORD; I sing for joy at the work of your hands. How great are your works, O LORD, how profound your thoughts!" [5] God wants us, like the Psalmist, to sing for joy at his works. He wants us to stand back in wonder and amazement at his handiwork. And he wants us to join with all creation in worship and praise. It is impossible to be full of joy and wonder and, at the same time, not feel good about ourselves: rejoicing enhances self-esteem.

We are meant also to care about creation: we do not carry out our responsibilities primarily from a sense of duty, but because of love. Loving involves relationships, and for good relationships there has to be a sense of rapport and understanding. Perhaps our best role model is St. Francis of Assisi, who considered all creatures to be his brothers and sisters in God. Similarly, the Celtic Christians sought communion with creation in order to worship the Creator more fully. Caring is itself a form of worship, pleasing to God and blessing the soul of man.

When we are able to truly love all of God's creatures, when our souls expand to encompass the whole cosmos, then we will no longer be shut away in our own little world, with a limited range of feelings. We will be much more open and free. This opening up is vital because, just as we cannot love others until we have learned to love ourselves, so we cannot truly love and esteem ourselves until we have learned to embrace the entire created world.

How much thought have you given to creation? Are you carrying out your God-given task? Are you in tune with nature? In order to have a healthy sense of your self as an individual, you also have to be aware of your self in connection

101

with others — and with all created life. Remember, Adam (adamah) means "one with the earth". So practice looking around you and start appreciating, wondering, asking questions, and praising. As you do so, your soul will be enlarged and enriched, and you will find yourself dipping deeply into the wells of your creative ability.

The greatness of man's potential

God made man with the need and ability to create. This includes creativity of the mind — such as composing poetry, prose and music — and creating with our hands. The Bible is full of examples of man's creative ability. Crafts mentioned include drafting and designing, gardening, carpentry and work in metal and stone, painting and pottery, spinning, weaving, and embroidery.... When God commanded Moses to build the tabernacle in the wilderness — around which the entire sacrificial system was developed — God told him to call together a variety of craftsmen, designers, embroiderers and weavers, under the leadership of one to whom he had given special skills:

> Then Moses said to the Israelites, "See, the LORD has chosen Bezalel...and he has filled him with the Spirit of God, with skill, ability and knowledge in all kinds of crafts — to make artistic designs for work in gold, silver and bronze, to cut and set stones, to work in wood and to engage in all kinds of artistic craftsmanship." [6]

In our modern era, with its emphasis on mental skills, the ability to create with the hands has been downgraded, with a resulting erosion of self-esteem. We need to remind ourselves of the great value God places on all skills and abilities. Jesus was a carpenter — a craftsman. His creative ability in this field was not incidental, it was part of God's divine plan and purpose. In this, as in everything else, Jesus is our example.

God has given everyone gifts. No one is excluded. However, when self-esteem is low there is a tendency to think, I can't do anything. But, as Jesus made clear in the parable of the talents, God is offended when we say that we have no gifts, or that our gifts don't really amount to anything. And he is disappointed when we make no effort to enhance and make use of our gifts. The apostle Paul wrote, "We have different gifts, according to the grace given us." [7] And Peter similarly wrote,

> Each one should use whatever gift he has received to serve others, faithfully administering God's grace in its various forms. If anyone speaks, he should do it as one speaking the very words of God. If anyone serves, he should do it with the strength God provides, so that in all things God may be praised through Jesus Christ. [8]

103

Our Father applauds our accomplishments and rejoices when we succeed, as long as we don't hurt others in the process and we remember that our competence comes from him, so we do all for his glory. "Whatever you do, work at it with all your heart, as working for the Lord, not for men...." [9] God wants us to recognise that any creative act can be a ministry to him.

God not only wants us to recognise and value our own gifts, but also those of others. This is tied up with valuing creation. When we value the creations of others, we also value them. Often, however, through lack of interest or understanding, we do not appreciate as we should. For example, we may enjoy the beauty of a garden or work of art, but fail to appreciate the time, effort and skill involved in designing and creating it. People who have low self-esteem tend to boost themselves by depreciating others. Improving self-esteem, then, will make it easier to uplift and encourage others. And conversely, as we learn to value and appreciate others, and how to express our gratitude or admiration, we will find that we too are uplifted and encouraged to make use of our own gifts.

Have you been able to recognise and employ *your* gifts? Or have you listened to voices from the past telling you that you can't do anything, you're useless, you can't get anything right? Maybe the voices are more subtle. Perhaps your gifts and abilities were simply ignored or overlooked because they didn't happen to be your parents' choices. When parents want children to fulfil their own frustrated ambitions, it is soul-destroying. In order to enhance your soul, it is vital that you discover *your* talents and pursue *your* interests. If you don't know what your interests are, think about anything you have enjoyed doing, from your school-days onwards. Do some brainstorming: write down anything that comes to mind. Then, from your list select some possibilities.

Having discovered your creative abilities, they must have an outlet. If you are so busy that you have no time for hobbies — interests that are pursued for their intrinsic value — then you are too busy. Creativity should also find expression in your working life, and this is more likely if you also do things just for fun. But in order to fully express your creativity, you must also constantly work at enriching your soul, feeding it with beauty and light.

ENRICHING THE SOUL

Absorbing beauty

The soul thrives on beauty because it was made for beauty. We are told to think about things that are true, noble, right, pure, lovely, admirable, excellent and praiseworthy. [10] And we cannot think about such things if we have never experienced them. When God made Adam and Eve, he placed them in a garden, in a scene of beauty. If you imagine the most beautiful, the most colourful, the sweetest-smelling and most restful garden in the world, your imagination will fall short of what the Garden of Eden must have been like before the Fall. Beauty is of God.

In order to experience beauty, we can begin by filling our souls with the beauty of God's creation: clouds floating across an azure sky, snow-capped mountains, the sea swirling around grey rocks, cool green forests, gardens ablaze with flowers.... When God led David in green pastures, beside the still waters, it restored his soul. Beauty not only enriches, it is also healing and soothing.

We can also experience beauty, and so enrich and restore our souls, by enjoying the beauty of man's creation: a painting, sculpture, a piece of embroidery, a dried-flower arrangement, a poem or piece of prose.... The list is endless. God has given us so many beautiful things to enjoy, and it grieves him if we do not take pleasure in his gifts, just as a loving parent would be disappointed in a child's disinterest or rejection of a long-planned, carefully chosen and expensive present.

As you enjoy the beauty of the world around, whether the magnificence of nature or the product of man's ingenuity, you will become increasingly aware of God's amazing diversity. And you will experience, in a more profound way, God as light. Without light there could be no colour — and no beauty. As you stop to ponder this amazing thought, you will also become increasingly aware of God's greatness, and of your own smallness in comparison. This awareness is humbling and, paradoxically, will give you a greater sense of self-worth. This, in turn, will enable you to become more in tune with yourself, and with the song of all creation.

Enjoying music

Music has a powerful impact on the soul. It can be the music of creation: the sound of the wind in the trees, the rustle of leaves, a bird's song. Or it can be the sound of silence: music that is heard only in the soul and that comes from being in synch with the rest of creation; our hearts beating to the rhythm of the universe. Or, it can be the music of the voice, of a musical instrument, an orchestra.... Music can lift the spirits, and even bring down the power of God.

In the Bible, music was used for entertainment, celebration or mourning, and worship. And a wide variety of instruments was used. God commands us to sing and make music in our hearts, in order to bless ourselves and each other. "Speak to one another with psalms, hymns and spiritual songs. Sing and make music in your heart to the Lord...." [11] Music is of God, although, like anything else, it can be distorted or misused. Music should never be intrusive, but respect the soul's need for stillness — and space.

Creating space

As well as beauty and music, the soul needs space, not just a broader view of God, his creation and man's potential, but room for its own growth and development. Ideally, the soul needs physical space, which is not always possible to find with today's mushrooming population and crowded cities. Even in the countryside the land is being despoiled in order to grow more and more surplus produce. Lack of space cuts us off from creation, so although we are physically crammed closer together, we actually become isolated: "Woe to you who add house to house and join field to field till no space is left and you live alone in the land." [12]

The soul also needs emotional space, which is connected with the need to rest. If we are constantly thinking about our anxieties and worries, or about things we have to do, or if we are frantically cramming our minds with information, the soul becomes cramped and its growth stunted. We can create space by allowing ourselves time to sit and quietly contemplate the scene before us, or to simply let our minds wander. People who have been abused tend to daydream excessively in order to escape reality, and this is detrimental to everyday living. But day-dreaming in order to rest our souls, to allow creative thoughts to germinate and blossom, is essential.

How much and how often do you fill your soul with beauty and music and allow it creative space? Maybe you have thought that this was indulgent. And if you live in a built-up area and have sometimes longed for open spaces and green fields, perhaps you have rebuked yourself, telling yourself that you should be contented with your lot. It is true that often in life we don't get what we need or want, and a spirit of contentment is essential in order to cope and prevent the onset of bitterness and despair. But your craving for beauty and space is, in fact, a natural and God-given cry from the depth of your being. Therefore, you should heed this cry and, as much as possible, try to satisfy your soul. If you starve it you will damage your self-esteem, whereas by meeting your soul's emotional and aesthetic needs, you will develop your sensing self, enabling it to grow and blossom.

SUMMARY

The soul is the essential, indefinable part of the self; it is the life principle, the seat of emotions and the source of creativity. In today's high-tech world the soul is often neglected and its growth stunted. This is because we have a shrunken God and a shrunken world, and man has shrunk himself. We need to enlarge our souls through discovering the greatness and wonder of God, who fills eternity and permeates all of creation, and whose story is told in so many different ways; and through discovering and appreciating our own talents and realising our potential.

In order to enlarge our souls' creative ability, they need constant enriching, through exposure to beauty, whether it be the loveliness of God's created world or of human creativity. They can also be enriched through the enjoyment of good music, and through creating emotional — and, if possible, physical — space. It is essential also that we work at discovering our own soul's individual shape, rather than trying to fit into a mould. We must be ourselves.

8

Self-esteem: the religious self (spirit)

OUR CONCEPT OF GOD

Where our concept of God comes from
The spirit ("pneuma", literally "breath") is that part of man which causes him to reach out to God and enables him to commune with God. Because our self-identity as Christians is based first and foremost on our relationship with God, any damage to the spirit will adversely affect all other aspects of the self. The spirit is damaged when we deny the existence of God, deny our need of God, or have a distorted image of God.

Although the true concept of God comes from the Bible, we actually see God as being like our own parents, in particular fathers. And since no human father is perfect, everyone, to some extent, has a distorted view of God. For those fortunate enough to have had a loving, godly father, the distortions will be minimal; but for those brought up by an abusive or neglecting father, the false images of God may be all-pervasive — in spite of knowing what the Bible teaches about God's character and ways of relating to man.

To a lesser extent, our concept of God comes from other authority figures, especially church leaders and Sunday school teachers. As God's earthly representatives they are meant to show us what God is like. Therefore, if they have let us down in any way or, worse, abused us, God's reflection will be dulled or deformed, and we will suffer accordingly.

Our concept of God comes also from our church and it's teaching. False doctrine will, of course, adversely affect the way we see God. But we can also produce a god of our own design, the creation of our own sinful minds, either to compensate for

108

negative experiences of a father-figure, or to accord with a chosen lifestyle that is actually displeasing to God.

The true concept of God

The only true representative of God is Jesus. The writer of Hebrews said, "The Son is the radiance of God's glory and the exact representation of his being...." [1] Jesus himself said this when he explained to Thomas, "If you really knew me, you would know my Father as well." [2] He said similarly to Philip, "Anyone who has seen me has seen the Father." [3] We know the Father through his Word and creation, and an innate knowledge of truth. But we see God in action, relating to humans, primarily through Jesus, and we start getting to know Jesus when we first come to him in repentance, accepting through faith his sacrifice for sin on the cross of Calvary. The more we know Jesus, the more our misconceptions about the Father will be rectified.

Misconceptions of God and idolatry

Distortions of God, whether they arose from our experience of a father, mother, teacher or significant other, or from our own imagination, are a form of idolatry; a violation of the second commandment:

> You shall not make for yourself an idol
> in the form of anything in heaven above
> or on the earth beneath or in the waters
> below. You shall not bow down to them
> or worship them; for I, the LORD your
> God, am a jealous God.... [4]

As Packer notes in his book, *Knowing God*, the second commandment doesn't just refer to the making and worship of gods other than Jahweh, otherwise it would merely be a repeat of the first: "You shall have no other gods before me." [5] Rather, it refers to the worship of the true God reduced to the form of an image — any kind of image, mental (imagination) or graven.

God is particularly vehement about violation of the second commandment, for several reasons. First, it is dishonouring to

God. It brings him down to our level. Secondly, it is misleading. Any image, mental or graven, focuses on only one aspect of God. For example, the golden calf depicted only God's strength. It said nothing about his love, purity, or other attributes. And thirdly, it is detrimental to our spiritual well-being. The very inadequacy of idols perverts our thoughts of God, and ultimately of ourselves. God wants us to know him as he really is, and to worship him in spirit and in truth.

Perhaps you have never stopped to consider if your perception of God is distorted. And maybe you have never thought that mental images may be as much idolatry as graven images. But do not let any new realisation of a false concept lead you to fear God's retribution — this itself is a distortion. Good human parents do not punish their children for misunderstanding or making mistakes, and neither does God. In the case of the children of Israel, their idolatry was not due to misunderstanding — although they had been influenced by the gods of Egypt — but to wilful disobedience. If you are aware of any possible misconceptions of God, it might be helpful to make a note of them now, before going on to the next section. Then add any newly discovered ones as you read on.

SOME COMMON DISTORTIONS OF GOD

God seen as absent

When an earthly father — or other significant person — has been absent, geographically or emotionally, it can lead to the greatest distortion of all: the belief that God doesn't exist, or that God is dead. Alternatively, God may be viewed as non-personal; an abstraction, totally unknowable and unreachable. More often, however, God is thought of as being unavailable. He's either somewhere else, busy with more important concerns; or he *is* there, but not really interested. When we think of God as absent, we react by telling ourselves, "It's impossible to know God, so I won't even try." Or, "I won't bother God with trivialities; I'll just pray in emergencies or when there's something major to discuss with him."

110

God may be thought of as being partially absent; he is unreliable, someone who cannot be trusted to do what he says he'll do. This inconsistency may be put down to fickleness, as well as disinterest, God being seen as someone who answers prayer only if he's in a good mood. The outcome of this distortion is to live in fear, never knowing if God is going to respond or not; or else to keep seeing how far we can push God, not really believing that he will carry out his threats.

Another result of having an absent earthly father is a tendency to think of God as absent-minded, so preoccupied with his own concerns that he is ignorant of what's going on in the world; someone who's out of touch. Our response to this distortion is to think that we can do what we like because God won't find out; or to think that we are better off without God because he's irrelevant.

It is difficult, if not impossible, to know and form a relationship with someone who is perceived as unavailable or absent. And with little or no knowledge of God, and an inability to get close to him, our spiritual development will be impaired, with inevitable lowering of self-esteem.

God seen as inadequate

When a human father or father figure has neglected a child's needs, the child feels unsafe and uncared for; and, as with the absent father, the experience of an inadequate parent can be transferred onto God. This gives rise to the false belief that God is unable to provide for our needs, or that he doesn't attempt to intervene when bad things happen. Our response to this distortion is to think, if God can't provide for me or protect me, then I'll do it myself — and I'll make sure that anyone who hurts me gets what's coming to him! Or, I'll help God out; he'll be glad of my assistance.

If we have experienced a father figure who failed to discipline us adequately, who was maybe even afraid to stand up to us, or a parent who was unable to deal with trouble generally, we may think of God as a wimp, someone weak in character, unable to control the world he has created. This distortion is likely to add to an already poor conscience development: there will be a further lowering of the standards God has set, and lack of true remorse when we fall short of those standards. At the same time, there is likely to be a sense of helplessness when we are confronted with evil; or conversely, a feeling that we have to take over and do God's work of punishing evil for him.

An inadequate God may also be seen as an indulgent God. This very common distortion leads to the belief that God's love is sentimental; that he likes to see us happy and will do anything we ask. The just, avenging God of the Old Testament doesn't exist. We are likely then to respond with thoughts such as, if I want something all I have to do is keep on pestering God, or bribe him, and I'll get it. Or, I can do what I like and get away with it.

It is impossible to trust someone who is perceived as inadequate. And as trust is the basis on which relationships are formed, this distortion too will prevent our forming a close bond with God. If we cannot feel secure in him, then, as with the absent God, our spirits will fail to reach out and connect with him, and self-esteem will be undermined.

God seen as abusive

Perhaps the most common distortion is to see God, not so much as absent or inadequate, but as abusive. When there has been physical mistreatment in childhood, there is a tendency to think of God as abusing, someone who is easily roused to anger, who is just waiting for us to put a foot wrong so that he can lash out, striking us down with some dreadful punishment. Our reaction, then, is to have an unhealthy fear of God, to be afraid of coming to him with problems and difficulties, and to live in a state of tension, terrified of making the smallest mistake. If we do go wrong, there will be a compulsion to hide. And, consciously or unconsciously, we may constantly punish ourselves so that God won't have to.

God may also be seen as emotionally abusing, someone who makes unrealistic demands on us, criticising us, putting us down, disapproving. God, then, is an exacting God, impossible to please. Our reaction to this distortion is to think that we're not good enough, that we can't measure up, and we may drive ourselves harder and harder, trying to win God's approval.

112

Or, we may decide that whatever we do, we'll never reach God's impossible standards, so we might as well give up.

Abuse may also take the form of control, so that we are not allowed to be ourselves but made to conform to someone else's expectations, and comply with their agendas. If we have experienced this kind of abuse in childhood, God may be seen as autocratic: a dictator or benevolent tyrant. A history of sexual abuse can similarly give rise to an image of God as intrusive, someone who allows us no privacy but violates our human rights and our need to be ourselves. One reaction to these distortions is to pray while not really believing that prayer will achieve anything because God is hard and immovable; he will do what he wants anyway. Or, we may pray for guidance for every triviality, either through an inability to make our own decisions, or fear of being out of God's will.

If we are afraid of God, thinking that he will abuse us in the way that human fathers or father figures have, through sadism, lack of control, or preoccupation with their own needs, then we cannot love him. Love is the opposite of fear and the two cannot co-exist. And without love there can be no self-development, and no true self-esteem.

Maybe *you* see God as abusive. And perhaps you have wondered why, in spite of trying to love and serve God, you feel as if you are wandering around in a wilderness. Or maybe you think of God as being absent; unapproachable or far away, so you cannot get to know him. Or is your God inadequate? Do you sometimes feel that he is exposing you to evil and failing to protect you, so you are unable to trust him? If any of these are your experience, then it comes from an earthly parent or guardian. This is not how God is. But do not condemn yourself for your misconceptions. When our experience of a father figure differs from the biblical concept of a Father God, then unfortunately it is our experience that has the most impact. So, in addition to working through your unhappy memories of childhood — perhaps with the help of a counsellor — and rejecting those negative views of self projected onto you by your abusers, saturate yourself with God's Word until the true concept of God displaces the false one. The Bible shows us in so many ways, as well as through Jesus, what God is really like.

WHAT GOD IS REALLY LIKE

God is omnipresent

God is not an absent God. He is everywhere. David wrote:

> Where can I go from your Spirit? Where can I flee from your presence? If I go up to the heavens, you are there; if I make my bed in the depths, you are there. If I rise on the wings of the dawn, if I settle on the far side of the sea, even there your hand will guide me, your right hand will hold me fast. [6]

This describes God's actual presence. But God is also depicted as being present symbolically: in the tabernacle, in Solomon's temple, with believers, and on the throne in heaven. The Bible also describes God's relational presence. God is far from the wicked, but he is near to those who seek him. Just as we can live with someone and feel a million miles apart, God can be there but not experienced as there. However, in the case of God, the distancing never comes from him. He is closer to us than breathing.

Not only is God's presence unrestricted geographically, it is also permanent, existing throughout eternity. And his faithfulness and truth endure through all generations. God is not an unreliable or inconsistent God. On the contrary, he has promised, "Never will I leave you; never will I forsake you." [7] And Jesus who, being God, is himself truth, promised, "And surely I am with you always, to the very end of the age." [8] We can have absolute trust in God's abiding presence. He is always there, whenever we need him.

God is also emotionally present: he knows our thoughts, how we feel at every moment, and he understands us perfectly. He is not an ignorant God. Rather, he is omniscient: all-knowing. His knowledge is so wide that he can name every one of the stars, and so specific that he can number the hairs on our head. We can hide nothing from the all-seeing God. The Psalmist wrote,

> O LORD, you have searched me and you
> know me. You know when I sit and when I
> rise; you perceive my thoughts from afar.
> You discern my going out and my lying
> down; you are familiar with all my ways.
> Before a word is on my tongue you know
> it completely, O LORD. [9]

God is with us always, wherever we are and whatever we are going through. This is because he is not just someone out there, but also someone in there. By his Spirit he dwells within. He is a part of us so he cannot help but be with us emotionally: heart, mind and soul. The knowledge that our heavenly Father loves us so much that he cannot stay away from us, that he actually deigns to live inside us, under our skin, is mind-boggling. And when we grasp the amazing truth of God in us, how can we possibly have low self-esteem!

God is omnipotent

As well as being all-knowing, God is also all-powerful. There is absolutely nothing that God cannot do. And he can do everything without effort; he never gets tired or weary. So he is definitely not an inadequate God. Jeremiah, wrote, "Ah, Sovereign LORD, you have made the heavens and the earth by your great power and outstretched arm. Nothing is too hard for you." [10] God is more than able to supply our physical needs of food, clothes, shelter, or any other requirement: "And my God will meet all your needs according to his glorious riches in Christ Jesus." [11] He is also more than able to protect us from anything that comes against us. He is our shield, our rock, and our strength.

Not only is God powerful enough to meet our needs and protect us, he is also able to deal with our wrongdoings, thus protecting us from ourselves. And he is able to deal with evil generally. God is not a wimp. On the contrary, he is strong in character, holy and just. And he disciplines his children fairly and consistently. The writer of Hebrews, quoting Proverbs, said, "My son, do not make light of the Lord's discipline, and do not lose heart when he rebukes you, because the Lord disciplines those he loves...." [12] As for the wicked, God will not let them go unpunished. His holiness and justice demand retribution. Such is God's power that he can even use evil for his own purposes, as he did with Joseph after his brothers threw him into the pit. "And we know that in all things God works for the good of those who love him...." [13]

At times it may seem that God is incapable of supplying our needs, or protecting us, because he doesn't give us what we want or think we need. But God is not an indulgent God. His love is tough love. He will give his children every good thing; but, in his wisdom, he will not pamper to our whims.

> "For my thoughts are not your thoughts, neither are your ways my ways," declares the LORD. "As the heavens are higher than the earth, so are my ways higher than your ways and my thoughts than your thoughts." [14]

Since God's thoughts and ways are so much higher than ours, he uses his power to our best advantage. He provides all we need and protects us from ourselves, as well as from those who would harm us, turning evil to good. And his love is strong enough to withstand our childish demands and tantrums when we don't get our own way. God's power enables him to give us exactly what we need to develop into mature Christians with a positive, healthy self-esteem. And he gives us exactly what we need because he is good.

God is good

Unlike many human fathers, God is loving and kind. He is not an abusing God. Although he disciplines us as children, he does this to facilitate our growth and development, not to harm us. God hates to see his children hurt; he wants instead to see us happy and blessed, and he is so overflowing with goodness that we need only ask and he will shower us with every good thing, far more than we can ever imagine. As the perfect Father, God meets not only our basic physical needs, but also our emotional needs for love, acceptance, approval and a sense of worth. The Psalmist wrote,

> Praise the LORD, O my soul; all my innermost being, praise his holy name. Praise the LORD, O my soul, and forget not all his benefits — who forgives all your sins and heals all your diseases, who redeems your life from the pit and crowns you with love and compassion, who satisfies your desires with good things so that your youth is renewed like the eagle's. [15]

God's goodness rejuvenates us, and his lovingkindness is a healing balm, soothing our hurts. Our heavenly Father is not waiting to hit us, but to hug us.

God's goodness is also manifested in patience and long-suffering. He is not an exacting God, impossible to please.

He who made us knows what to expect of us, and he makes allowances for our being human. His compassion never fails. This is demonstrated through Jesus, who is God incarnate. Jesus understands us and is patient with us because, as a man, he was tempted in all the ways that we are, yet he remained without sin. Far from being demanding and emotionally abusing, God helps us express our innermost feelings, then he responds to those feelings, enabling us to develop sound minds and hearts and grow into spiritual maturity.

God's goodness is also humble and considerate. He is not an autocratic God. On the contrary, his instructions are always gentle. Jesus said,

> "Come to me, all you who are weary and
> burdened, and I will give you rest. Take
> my yoke upon you and learn from me, for
> I am gentle and humble in heart, and you
> will find rest for your souls. For my yoke
> is easy and my burden is light." [16]

God's humility brings him down to our level; he walks beside us as he did, prior to the Fall, with Adam in the Garden of Eden. His very name, Immanuel, means "God with us"; that is, God who walks alongside us. And he listens carefully to what we have to say, as he did when Abraham was pleading for the life of his nephew in Sodom. He does not inflict his will on us. From the beginning of time God's divine, unchanging will has allowed for man's free will. This is a paradox and difficult for us humans to grasp, but we can believe and accept that prayer does change things. God's love is not dictatorial, but liberating. He wants us to develop and grow into his fullness, which we can do only if we are allowed to grow in our own time and in our own way.

God, then, is your perfect parent. He is not an absent Father, so you can get to know him and get close to him. He is not an inadequate Father, so you can trust him. He is not an abusing Father, so you can love him. He is ever-present, he is all knowing and all powerful, and he is good. His goodness never fails, and his love endures forever. As you work at clearing away any distortions about God, through recognising how they arose, facing up to and dealing with past hurts, and getting to know God as he really is, read Psalm 136 and fill your mind with this wonderful truth:

HIS LOVE ENDURES FOREVER!

GETTING TO KNOW GOD

Studying his Word

In order to fully know, trust and love God, we have to know what he is really like and experience him as he truly is. We commence by replacing the mental distortions with truth, as revealed in Scripture. And, since the distortions have usually formed in childhood and, over the years, sunk deep into our soul and spirit, a mere superficial reading of Scripture is not enough.

We have to study God's Word, write his Word on our hearts, repeat it, memorise it, reflect on it, and apply it. Also, in order to see the whole picture, avoiding a one-sided view of God, we must study the whole of God's Word, from Genesis to Revelation. Since Jesus is God's perfect representative, showing us what the Father is like, the initial focus should be on the Gospels. As you get to know God as Father, you will find it increasingly easier to come to him as Father.

Coming to the Father

We come to the Father through prayer, that is, through open and honest communication with God. We are told to pray humbly, with thanksgiving, and to pray continuously. This does not mean repeating non-stop prayers, but living in an atmosphere of prayer, and developing the habit of chatting to God as we go about our daily work. We must also develop a spirit of submission so that we come to the Father in obedience. His commands are not arduous; they are summed up in the exhortation to love God with all our heart, soul and mind, and our neighbour as ourselves. And loving is easy when we feel loved.

In order to know God as Father we must also learn to be childlike — which is not the same as childish. Jesus said that unless we become like little children, we will never enter the kingdom of heaven. This means that we must develop their characteristics. Little children are trusting, eager to learn and quick to imitate; they respond to love and they want to please; they are innocent; they enjoy life and have fun; and they grow. Little children become big children, and big children become adults — as you will, emotionally and spiritually, as you love and learn from your Father in heaven.

Learning from God's representatives

As we become closer to God, and more in tune with him, we will find ourselves being drawn to godly and loving people who can demonstrate further what God is like, and facilitate deeper healing from childhood abuse and neglect. The apostle Paul wrote, regarding the importance of God's representatives, "Join with others in following my example, brothers, and take note of those who live according to the pattern we gave you." [17] Peter wrote similarly to his fellow elders, to be an example on earth of what God is like.

As you learn about and experience God in truth, whether through his Word, through prayer, or the example of God-like others, you will find yourself growing to be like him. Then you yourself will become his representative, an example of his holiness, goodness and patience. It is once again the pattern of love: the more you experience love the more you will be able to demonstrate love. There can be no greater self-esteem than that which comes from knowing assuredly that you are so filled with love that it is overflowing to others.

Self-esteem, then, which is linked with self-love, begins and ends with God. It starts with our being created in his image, wonderfully made with gifts and abilities to use for his glory and the benefit of all creation; and with our becoming God's adopted children and heirs through Christ's gift of redemption. It ends when we are made perfect in love, having completed our journey through life, restored and healed of all those hurts that have distorted our views of God, the world and ourselves. Adam was made with perfect self-esteem, and we are meant to have perfect self-esteem, through rediscovering our roots and roles in God — through the way of humility.

SUMMARY

Although our concept of God comes primarily from the Bible, we tend to see him as being like our own fathers, or other significant adults in our childhood. So, if we haven't had a father, or our experience of a father or father figure has been harmful, through having been abused or neglected, then we will have a more distorted view of God than those who have had a good upbringing. We may see God as being geographically or emotionally absent, as being inadequate in some way, or autocratic and abusing.

In order to correct the distortions, we must first recognise that they exist; that we may not be seeing God as he really is.

Then we must seek to know God in truth, discovering him to be always present, all-powerful and all-knowing, loving, good and kind, as well as holy and just. We get to know God through Bible study, prayer, the example of godly men and women, and through opening up to God, allowing him to demonstrate his compassion and understanding. God is the perfect Father, one who loves us unconditionally, accepts us, values us, essentially approves of us, and lovingly disciplines us, changing us into his likeness. Becoming like God means becoming perfect in love, and therefore having perfect self-esteem: a sense of self that is humbly thankful that God has made us just the way we are.

REVIEW
How to improve your self-esteem

1. Recognise that low self-esteem is displeasing to God, and why; discover those areas in which your self-esteem is most lacking, and how significant people in your childhood have helped form your self-esteem. Reject their negative views of you — but be honest with yourself. Stop putting yourself down. Focus on who you are, and who you are becoming, in God.

2   Recognise and accept that you are God's child through creation and redemption — Christ having died for you on the cross of Calvary — and that you are greatly beloved, essentially good, valuable, accepted, approved and entrusted with great responsibility. Take your stewardship of creation seriously. Practice acting like God's child: trusting, spontaneous and eager to please. Discover the implications of being a chosen people, a holy nation and a royal priesthood.

3. Discover your personal identity. Become more aware of how your national, cultural, ecclesiastical and personal family history have helped made you the way you are. Be proud of the positive, and accept the negative as also being part of you. Work through, maybe with help, the pain of rejection or abuse, and find ways of turning evil into good. Consider your identity as it is reflected in your name, attributes, gender, roles and relationships. Know what you believe and why, and increase awareness of your values and interests. Set goals and strive to reach them.

4. Work at developing the social self (heart). Start responding to God's love, and learn to love everyone and everything, including yourself. Begin to accept love from others; learn to gracefully accept compliments and praise, and thankfully receive offers of practical help and demonstrations

123

of affection. Improve your social life: if you tend to be reclusive, get out more and make an effort to make new friends. Develop the friendships you already have. Learn some social skills. Practice being assertive.

5.   Work at developing the thinking self (mind). Accept that God has given you a brain, and use it to explore God's Word and works, which means any subject under the sun, or beyond. Question and challenge any lack of interest or motivation. Stimulate your curiosity and sense of wonder. Beginning with your interests, question, check out, test, prove and discover. Open yourself up to new experiences. Set realistic goals and achieve them by learning new skills and developing new abilities. Take pride in your achievements.

6.   Work at improving the physical self (body). Recognise any misconceptions about your body, and challenge them. Start seeing your body as God sees it, and respect it accordingly. Improve your health: go on a diet, take up some form of exercise, learn to relax. Enhance your appearance through better posture and paying attention to clothes and general grooming. Recognise your good points and enhance them; play down the not so good ones. Enjoy colour and beauty as gifts of God. Offer your body as a pleasing sacrifice to God.

7.   Work at enhancing the sensing self (soul). Expand your soul by recognising how great God is and how little we know him. Develop an appreciation for God's creation and man's gifts and abilities. Discover your own talents, and employ them. Use all five senses to look and observe, hear, smell, taste and touch. Find new hobbies and interests. Be aware of your feelings and learn to control and express them constructively. Enrich your soul by exposing it to beauty and music, and allowing it space. Stop trying to fit into someone else's mould. Discover your own unique-ness, and let your true inner self find free expression.

8. Work at developing the religious self (spirit). Recognise any distorted views of God, and correct them through finding God as he is revealed in Scripture, demonstrated by Christ, and manifested through creation. Stop limiting God; allow your perceptions of him to expand. Stand firm on the foundation of God's Word, but be flexible and open to new ideas. Trust your spiritual judgment. Develop a healthy conscience, one that is neither too lax nor too harsh. Learn from your mistakes and forgive yourself. Count your blessings, and be humbly thankful that God has made you the way you are.

QUESTIONNAIRE TO ASSESS YOUR
SELF-ESTEEM LEVEL

The following is meant only as a rough guide, to help you discover those areas of self-esteem in which you are struggling most and on which you need to do the most work. Answer each question, grading yourself 1-5 as follows:

1. No, definitely not
2. No, not really
3. Sometimes/some aspects
4. Yes, a little
5. Yes, very much so

Then, total your score and mark yourself out of 200; the higher the score the healthier your self-esteem.

Self-Identity
1. Can you accept that God loves you unconditionally?
2. Are you fulfilling your role as steward of creation?
3. Are you proud of your nationality and culture?
4. Do you feel a valuable member of the Church?
5. Do you feel part of your family?
6. Are you happy with your gender?
7. Does your job reflect your values and interests?

The Social Self (Heart)
8. Are you able to form close relationships?
9. Can you express feelings and show affection?
10. Can you accept love and affection from others?
11. Can you accept practical help from others?
12. Are you able to tolerate others' weaknesses?

The Thinking Self (Mind)

13. Do you believe that you have intelligence?
14. Do you have a sense of curiosity and wonder?
15. Do you have a wide variety of interests?
16. Are you satisfied with your achievements?
17. Are you genuinely happy when others achieve?

The Physical Self (Body)

18. Do you like your body?
19. Do you look after your body?
20. Do you take pride in your appearance?
21. Are you able to enjoy sex?
22. Can you give and accept compliments on appearance?

The Sensing Self (Soul)

23. Do you make full use of all your senses?
24. Are you comfortable with your feelings?
25. Are you using your creativity?
26. Do you appreciate beauty?
27. Are you able to relax and have fun?

The Religious Self (Spirit)

28. Do you love God?
29. Can you relate to God as a loving Father?
30. Can you express negative feelings to God?
31. Can you trust God in all circumstances?
32. Do you feel that you are growing spiritually?

General growth and development

33. Are you open to new ideas?
34. Do you welcome new experiences?
35. Do you take responsibility for your mistakes?
36. Can you calmly accept constructive criticism?
37. Are you able to deal with conflict?
38. Can you feel sure of yourself without others' approval?
39. Do you give yourself credit for your successes?
40. Do you feel capable of change?

SOME EXERCISES TO DISCOVER
YOUR IDENTITY

The following list of exercises is not fully comprehensive; it is intended only to get you started. You may add any items that have been omitted, such as who you are with regard to creation, or in connection with your cultural heritage. Write as little or as much as you like.

1.   List at least six aspects of your identity based on who you are in God, under the heading, "I am…". For example, "I am God's child", "I am a treasure".

2.   List at least six aspects of your identity based on who you are historically, under the headings, "I am...", or "I was brought up as…". For example, "I am British", "I was brought up as an Anglican".

3.   List at least six things that your parents' history tells you about yourself, under the headings, "My mother...", or "My father...". For example, "My mother is musical", or "My father didn't believe in women going out to work".

4.   List at least six things that your name and gender tell you about yourself, under the headings, "I am...", or "I was...". For example, "I was named after my great aunt because Mum hoped to inherit from her", or, "I'm a disappointment to Dad because he wanted me to be a boy".

5.   List at least six relational roles, under the heading, "I am...". For example, "I am a wife", "I am a father".

6. List at least six occupational roles, under the headings, "I am...", or "I used to be...". For example, "I am a builder", "I used to be a nurse".

7. List at least six beliefs and norms (ethics) under the heading, "I believe in...". For example, "I believe in God", "I believe in freedom of speech".

8. List at least six values under the heading, "Things important to me are...". For example, "my family", "having a job", "being loved", "being a success".

9. List at least six hobbies or interests under the headings, "I am interested in...", or "I enjoy...". For example, "I am interested in local history", "I enjoy stamp collecting".

10. List at least six goals under the heading, "I would like...". For example, "I would like to be a more patient mother", "I would like to learn how to ski".

SELFTALK: IDEAS FOR POSITIVE THINKING

We are told that, as a person thinks in his heart, so is he.[1] The way you think, and talk to yourself, will influence how you behave and determine the kind of person you will ultimately become. So it is important that you become aware of, and learn to control, your internal speech.

We speak at the rate of two to three hundred words per minute, but think at the rate of three to four thousand words per minute. So, how you talk to yourself has ten times the impact of how others talk to you. If you keep putting yourself down while others are praising and encouraging you, you will defeat their good intentions every time.

The following are some common self put-downs that must be challenged if you are to develop a healthy self-esteem.

Thoughts about God and creation
1.   I am not very important to God.
2.   I'm too bad, stupid, ugly, for God to love me.
3.   I don't have any gifts I can use for God.
4.   What I think and do can have little or no effect on creation.

Tell yourself:
1.   *I am important to God because I am his child.*
2.   *God loves me, just as I am.*
3.   *God has given me gifts and abilities that I can and must use for him*
4.   *I might be only one little individual, but my thoughts and actions can have major repercussions.*

Thoughts about myself and others
1. Other people don't like me or want me unless I work at pleasing them.
2. I have to be approved by others to be happy.
3. I don't have anything worth saying.
4. I don't measure up: others are more attractive, more intelligent.

Tell yourself:
1. *I am likeable, just as I am; it's not necessary or realistic to expect everyone to like me. (Not everyone liked Jesus.)*
2. *I can be happy as long as I approve of myself.*
3. *I do have things worth saying; my opinions are valid.*
4. *I don't have to compare myself with others, just work at being the best I can be.*

Thoughts about myself and my personal development
1. I'm ugly, unattractive, fat. It's not worth making an effort with my appearance.
2. I'm too stupid to learn anything.
3. I can't get anything right.
4. I'll never amount to anything.

Tell yourself:
1. *I am not ugly or unattractive. If I am overweight, I can work at this; I'm worth it.*
2. *God gave me a brain, and I can learn if I put my mind to it.*
3. *It doesn't matter about always getting things right. I don't have to be perfect.*
4. *I can and will achieve something in life.*

ENDNOTES

Chapter 1

1   Romans 8: 15
2   Romans 8: 1
3   Luke 3: 8
4   Ecclesiastes 3: 11
5   Colossians 1: 21-23
6   1 John 3: 1
7   Matthew 22: 39

Chapter 2

1   Matthew 22: 37
2   1 Thessalonians 5: 23
3   Romans 8: 16
4   Genesis 1: 1
5   Colossians 1: 15-17
6   John 4: 24
7   James 1: 18
8   Galatians 3: 26
9   Romans 8: 23
10   1 Peter 2: 9-10
11   Psalm 8: 4-8
12   Psalm 24: 1
13   Genesis 3: 17
14   Hosea 4: 1-3
15   John 3: 16
16   Romans 8: 21
17   Isaiah 65: 25

Chapter 3

1   Deuteronomy 32: 7
2   Colossians 2: 8
3   Psalm 27: 10
4   Luke 2: 30

Chapter 4

1   Luke 7: 47
2   John 14: 15
3   Proverbs 27: 6
4   1 Corinthians 13: 4-8

Chapter 5

1   Colossians 3: 10
2   Luke 17: 32
3   Philippians 2: 5
4   2 Timothy 2: 15
5   Romans 1: 20
6   2 Timothy 3: 16-17
7   Hebrews 4: 12
8   Psalm 19: 1-4
9   Psalm 111: 2

Chapter 6

1   Romans 7: 18
2   Mark 7: 21-23
3   Ephesians 4: 17
4   1 Samuel 16: 7
5   Psalm 139: 13-14
6   1 Timothy 4: 8
7   1 Timothy 4: 3
8   Psalm 104: 14-15
9   Proverbs 27: 9
10   Proverbs 31: 21-22
11   1 Corinthians 6: 19-20
12   Romans 12: 1

Chapter 7

1   2 Chronicles 6: 18
2   Jeremiah 23: 24
3   Romans 1: 19-20
4   Job 42: 3
5   Psalm 92: 4-6
6   Exodus 35: 30-33
7   Romans 12: 6
8   1 Peter 4: 10-11
9   Colossians 3: 23
10   Philippians 4: 8
11   Ephesians 5: 19
12   Isaiah 5: 8

Chapter 8

1	Hebrews 1: 3	11	Philippians 4: 19
2	John 14: 7	12	Hebrews 12: 5-6
3	John 14: 9	13	Romans 8: 28
4	Exodus 20: 4-5	14	Isaiah 55: 8-9
5	Exodus 20: 3	15	Psalm 103: 1-5
6	Psalm 139: 7-10	16	Matthew 11: 28-30
7	Hebrews 13: 5	17	Philippians 3: 17
8	Matthew 28: 20		
9	Psalm 139: 1-4	**Selftalk**	
10	Jeremiah 32: 17	1	Proverbs 23: 7
			(King James Version)

SCRIPTURE REFERENCES
FOR FURTHER STUDY
In the order mentioned in the text

Chapter 1

Our inheritance as children: Galatians 3: 26, 29; 1 Peter 1: 3-5

Our need to grow as children: 1 Peter 2: 2; 2 Peter 3: 18

Confidence to approach God: Hebrews 4: 15-16

Created in God's image: Genesis 1: 27

Responsible for creation: Genesis 1: 26-30; 2: 15; Psalm 8: 3-8;
   Hebrews: chapters 2 and 7

Of value to God: Matthew 6: 25-26; 13: 44-46

Accepted and approved by God: Genesis 1: 27 –31; Ephesians 2: 10

Loved and loveable: John 3: 16; Ephesians 2: 4-5; 1 John 3: 1; 4: 9-10

Chapter 2

Our resurrection bodies: 1 Corinthians 15: 35-58; Philippians 3: 20-21

God's love: Ephesians 3: 16-19

Communication with God: Romans 8: 16; 2 Corinthians 13: 14

The earth is God's: Leviticus 25: 23;

Creation inherently good: Genesis 1: 31; 1 Timothy 4:4

Creation upheld: Acts 17: 28; 1 Corinthians 8: 6; Hebrews 1: 2-3

Worshipping with/for creation: Psalm 104; Psalm 148

Effects of the Fall: Romans 3: 23; 5: 12

Effects reversed by Christ: Romans 5: 19; 1 Corinthians 15: 21-22

Chosen before creation: Ephesians 1: 4

Chosen to be kings and priests: Revelation 1: 5-6

Partakers of a new covenant: 1 Corinthians 11: 23-26; Hebrews 9: 13-22

Chapter 3

The Church's foundation: Matt. 16: 18; Ephesians 2: 19-22; 1 Peter 2: 4-8

Tradition and customs: Matthew 15: 3; Luke 4: 16; Acts 28: 17

Biblical names: Genesis 3: 20; 5: 29; 10: 25

Importance of names: Isaiah 40: 26; Luke 10: 20; John 10: 3; Rev. 3: 12

Knowing our beliefs: 1 Peter 3: 15

Chapter 4

God's love passing knowledge: Psalm 139; Ephesians 3: 19

God's command to love:

   himself: Matthew 22: 37

   our neighbour: Leviticus 19: 18, 34; Matthew 22: 39; Luke 10: 25-37

   our relatives: Ephesians 5: 25,33; 1 Timothy 5: 4,8

   fellow believers: John 13: 34-35; 15: 12-17; 1 John 4: 7-12, 19-21

   our enemies: Matthew 5: 43-48; Luke 6: 32

Not good to be alone: Genesis 2: 18

Not left alone: Psalm 27: 10

Chapter 5

Created to think and assess: Genesis 2: 19
Intended to be wise: Proverbs 3: 13; Proverbs 10: 14
Intended to test and prove: Psalm 34: 8; Malachi 3: 10
Intended to love with our mind: Luke 10: 27
Using mind: Matt. 1: 19; Mk. 14: 72; Acts 17: 11; 18: 4; 1 Pet. 3: 15-16
Inspiration of Scripture: Hebrews 1: 1; 2 Peter 1: 20-21
God revealed through creation: Psalm 104
Rejoicing in God's world: Psalm 92: 4

Chapter 6

God's creation good: Genesis 1: 31; Ephesians 2: 10; 1 Timothy 4: 4
Need for rest: Exodus 20: 10; 34: 21; Psalm 23: 2-3; Mark 6: 31
Need for food and clothes: Matthew 6: 25; Luke 12: 22-31
Avoiding gluttony: Philippians 3: 18-19
Beauty and adornment: Ezekiel 16: 1-2, 9-19; Psalm 45: 13-14;
   1 Corinthians 11: 15; 1 Timothy 2: 9-10; Revelation 19: 7
Conforming to the world: Romans 12: 2

Chapter 7

The greatness of God: 1 Kings 8: 27
Lamb slain from eternity: Revelation 13: 8
Jesus, revelation of the Father: Hebrews 1: 1-3
Jesus, example of mastery: John 13: 1-17; Philippians 2: 5-8
Learning from creation: Proverbs 6: 6-8
Appreciating creation: Job: chapters 38 and 39; Psalm 104
Using gifts: Matt. 25: 14-30; 1 Cor. 12: 27-31; 2 Cor 3: 5; Col 3: 23
Use of music: Ex. 15: 20-21; 1 Sam. 16: 15-23; 2 Chron. 5: 12-14;
   Psalm 137: 1-4; Psalm 150; Colossians 3: 16

Chapter 8

Idolatry: Exodus 32; Isaiah 40: 18-24
God is truth: Numbers 23: 19; John 4: 24; 14: 6; 17: 17
God's presence: Exodus 40: 33-38; 1 Kings 8: 27; Proverbs 15: 29;
   Matthew 18: 20; James 4: 8; Revelation 21: 3
God's faithfulness: Psalm 119: 90; Malachi 3: 6
God's omniscience: Ps. 147: 4-5; Lk. 12: 7; Rom. 11: 33; 1 John 3: 20
God's omnipotence: Genesis 45: 4-8; Deut. 32: 35; Isaiah 40: 21-31;
   2 Thessalonians 1: 6-10; Hebrews 10: 30-31
God's supply: Matthew 7: 9-11; Ephesians 3: 20
God's empathy: Genesis 18: 16-33; Psalm 103: 8-14; Isaiah 7: 14;
   Lamentations 3: 22-23; Matt. 1: 23; Rom. 8: 26-27; Heb. 2: 14-18
God's representatives: 1 Peter 5: 1-4
Prayer: Matthew 18: 1-4; Luke 18: 10-14; Philippians 4: 6;
   1 Thessalonians 5: 17-18

SELECTED BIBLIOGRAPHY

Berkhof, Louis. *A Summary of Christian Doctrine*. 1938.
   Edinburgh: Banner of Truth, 1974.
Bulfinch, Thomas. *Bulfinch's Mythology*. 1855.
   New York: Avenel, 1979.
Coleman, James C., Butcher, James N. and Carson, Robert E. *Abnormal
   Psychology and Modern Life*. Glenview: Scott Foresman, 1980.
Douglas, J. D. (ed.) *The New Bible Dictionary*.
   London: Inter-Varsity, 1962.
Dowley, Tim. (ed.) *The History of Christianity*. Tring: Lion, 1982.
Frazer, James G. *The Golden Bough*. 1890. New York: Avenel, 1981.
Fromm, Erich. *The Art of Loving*. 1957. London: Thorsons, 1995.
Helfer, Ray E. and Kempe, C. Henry. (ed.) *Child Abuse and Neglect:
   The Family and the Community*. Cambridge: Ballinger, 1976.
Hummel, Charles E. *The Galileo Connection*.
   Downers Grove: Inter-Varsity, 1986.
Lewis, C. S. *Miracles*. 1947. London: Fontana, 1974.
Matthews, Victor H. *Manners and Customs in the Bible*. 1988.
   Revised edition, Peabody: Hendrickson, 1992.
Osborne, Cecil. *The Art of Understanding Yourself*.
   Grand Rapids: Zondervan, 1979.
Packer, J. I. *Knowing God*. London: Hodder, 1973.
Pagels, Elaine. *The Gnostic Gospels*. London: Penguin, 1979.
Russell, Colin A. *Cross-currents: Interactions between science and
   faith*. 1985. Grand Rapids: Eerdmans, 1985.
Staniforth, Maxwell. (trans.) *Early Christian Writings*.
   London: Penguin, 1967.
Strong, Thomas B. *A Manual of Theology*. 1892. London: Black, 1913.
Vine, W. E. *Vine's Expository Dictionary of New Testament Words*.
   Peabody: Hendrickson, no date.
Wilkinson, Loren. (ed.) *Earthkeeping in the Nineties*. 1980.
   Revised edition, Grand Rapids: Eerdmans, 1991.

INDEX

Also by Jennifer Minney

Will Jesus kick my ball back?

The amazing story of an adoption that should have been impossible, of cerebral palsy, and a child whose avid curiosity and irrepressible giggles have made him a joy and delight to many.

It is also the story of the author's spiritual and psychological journey — from a background of abuse and rejection, through years of infertility, to a place of trust in God's goodness, even when his long-promised child turns out to be severely brain-damaged. It is a story of learning how to open up to God's love and experiencing him, no longer as a rigid, punitive Father, but as a loving, approachable Father with whom it is safe to be oneself, to be child-like — to play.

The two stories blend as mother and child grow together, developing their full potential as she learns to love herself and a child whom a neurologist had written off.

This book has had a profound impact on those who have read it, provoking laughter, producing tears, challenging, uplifting and enriching the soul. It is a book that is hard to put down.

ISBN : 0-9538446-0-9

Available from bookshops or direct from:

> Silvertree Publishing (Dept SE)
> PO Box 2768
> Yeovil
> Somerset BA22 8XZ

£7.95 (postage and packing free in UK)

Also by Jennifer Minney

Song of Creation

Song of Creation is a beautifully illustrated collection of poems, grouped according to the seven days of creation, and glorifying God as Creator; with an eighth section on current environmental issues — creation in danger.

There are poems for every mood and need, such as the mind-expanding "What is sky?", the tongue-teasing "Fun fishes", the nostalgic "Dancing girl" and the restful "A day in the forest".

This anthology will enhance development of every aspect of the self: it will enlarge your heart and mind; it will touch and stir your soul; and, through increasing awareness of the beauty and diversity of the created world and our responsibility towards creation, it will enrich your spirit.

This is a book you will want to read again and again. It will also make a perfect gift for that special person in your life.

Available, from 2001, from bookshops or direct from:

Silvertree Publishing (Dept SE)
PO Box 2768
Yeovil
Somerset BA22 8XZ

Also by Jennifer Minney

Silvertree Gro-book series

The author (BA Hons, SRN, SCM) has combined Bible teaching and modern psychology to produce a series of booklets on common emotional problems that hinder personal growth and development.

Each booklet discusses causes, signs and symptoms, using Bible characters as examples, and provides guidelines for overcoming the immediate effects. The problems are also viewed in the context of the entire person, and the reader is helped to begin changing destructive patterns of thinking and behaviour; to move beyond the problem towards spiritual and psychological wholeness.

Titles as follows:

Beyond depression: Growing into light
Beyond anger: Growing into calm
Beyond stress: Growing into serenity
Beyond fear: Growing into faith
Beyond marital discord: Growing into love
Beyond parenting chaos: Growing into harmony

Available, from end 2000, from bookshops or direct from:

Silvertree Publishing (Dept SE)
PO Box 2768
Yeovil
Somerset BA22 8XZ